Study Guide

for use with

FOURTH CANADIAN EDITION

sociology
in our times

Diana Kendall · Jane Lothian Murray · Rick Linden

Prepared by DIANE SYMBALUK
GRANT MacEWAN COLLEGE

THOMSON

★

NELSON

Australia   Canada   Mexico   Singapore   Spain   United Kingdom   United States

THOMSON

NELSON

Study Guide for Use with Sociology in Our Times
Fourth Canadian Edition
Diana Kendall, Jane Lothian Murray, and Rick Linden

Prepared by Diane Symbaluk

Associate Vice President,
Editorial Director:
Evelyn Veitch

Publisher:
Joanna Cotton

Acquisitions Editor:
Cara Yarzab

Marketing Manager:
Lenore Taylor

Senior Developmental Editor:
Rebecca Rea

Production Editor:
Karri Yano

Proofreader:
Rodney Rawlings

Senior Production Coordinator:
Hedy Sellers

Design Director:
Ken Phipps

Cover Design:
Sasha Moroz

Cover Image:
Daly & Newton/Stone/
Getty Images

Compositor:
Daryn Dewalt

Printer:
Webcom

Library and Archives Canada Cataloguing in Publication

Symbaluk, Diane, 1967-
  Study guide for use with Sociology in our times, fourth Canadian edition/ prepared by Diane Symbaluk.

ISBN 0-17-610283-3

1. Sociology—Problems, exercises, etc. I. Title.

HM586.K45 2006 Suppl. 1   301
C2005-907869-3

TABLE OF CONTENTS

Preface

Objectives of the Study Guide

This Study Guide is designed to help you master the information contained in the fourth Canadian edition of Diana Kendall, Jane Lothian Murray, and Rick Linden's (2007) *Sociology in Our Times*. As a supplement, the Study Guide reinforces text materials and provides opportunities to apply what is being learned.

Organization of the Study Guide

Each chapter corresponds to a chapter in the text and contains the following:

I. *Chapter Outline:* The chapter outline provides topic headings and indicates materials covered in a given chapter.

II. *Chapter Summary:* The summary alerts you to key issues and provides you with a framework for organizing the materials contained in that chapter. You are encouraged to read through this section before and after you read the corresponding chapter in the text.

III. *Key Terms:* This section identifies key terms that are central to the topic under consideration. For study purposes, you might write out definitions for each of the terms and review them several times.

IV. *Key Terms Quiz:* This quiz tests identification and definition of the key terms.

V. *Key People:* This section indicates the theorists and researchers who contribute to main topics and ideas covered in the chapter.

VI. *Key People Quiz:* This quiz tests your ability to identify the contributions of key people from the chapter.

VII. *Learning Objectives:* These statements identify what you are expected to know from your reading of the chapter. You are encouraged to write detailed notes for each learning objective. Learning objectives likely form the basis of your examinations in this course.

VIII. *Unit Mastery Quizzes:* These quizzes test your understanding of the learning objectives. Multiple-choice questions test whether you can recall important ideas, define key terms, and/or apply sociological concepts in a meaningful way. True or false questions determine if you know about and understand key facts. Fill-in-the-blank statements are used to identify central issues and terms. Finally, matching problems help you connect concepts with their appropriate theoretical perspectives, originators, or key ideas.

IX. *Solutions to the Quizzes:* This section includes answers to all of the questions and exercises posed in the quizzes.

Suggestions for Using This Study Guide

1. Read over the chapter outline to familiarize yourself with the materials covered.
2. Skim over the chapter summary and then read that chapter in the textbook.
3. Expand on the chapter summary by taking notes and use the outline for headings.
4. Write out a definition for each of the key terms and include examples.
5. After studying the definitions, complete the review of key terms.
6. Write out the list of key people, indicating the major contribution of each person.
7. Test your knowledge by completing the review of key people.
8. List the 20 learning objectives and provide detailed answers to these items.
9. After reviewing the chapter and your notes, complete the unit mastery quiz.
10. Check your answers with those provided and review items with which you had difficulty.

The Sociological Perspective

Chapter Outline

Chapter Summary

Sociology is the systematic study of human society and social interaction. Sociology enables us to see how individual behaviour is largely shaped by the groups to which we belong and the society in which we live. The sociological imagination helps us to understand how seemingly personal troubles, such as suicide, actually are related to larger social forces such as cohesiveness in society. Sociology is moving toward a more global approach that takes into account challenges that face other nations, and the world at large.

Sociology emerged out of the social upheaval produced by industrialization and urbanization in the late eighteenth century. Some early social thinkers including Auguste Comte, Harriet Martineau, Herbert Spencer, and Emile Durkheim emphasized social order and stability; others including Karl Marx, Max Weber, and Georg Simmel focused on conflict and social change. From its origins in Europe, sociology spread to North America in the 1890s when departments of sociology were established at the University of Chicago and Atlanta University. The first sociology department in Canada was established in 1925 at McGill University in Montreal.

Sociologists use different theoretical perspectives to examine social life. Functionalist perspectives assume that society is a stable, orderly system. Conflict perspectives assume that society is a continuous power struggle among competing groups, often based on class, race, ethnicity, or gender. Feminist perspectives focus on the significance of gender in understanding and explaining inequalities that exist between men and women. Symbolic interactionist perspectives focus on how people make sense of their everyday social interactions. Finally, postmodern perspectives oppose the grand narratives used to explain modern thinking and examine societies as characterized by an information explosion, a rising consumer society, and the emergence of a global village.

Key Terms

alienation *(p. 14)*

anomie *(p. 13)*

bourgeoisie *(p. 14)*

class conflict *(p. 14)*

commonsense knowledge *(p. 4)*

conflict perspectives *(p. 22)*

dysfunctions *(p. 20)*

feminist perspectives *(p. 23)*

functionalist perspectives *(p. 20)*

global interdependence *(p. 4)*

industrialization *(p. 9)*

latent functions *(p. 20)*

macrolevel analysis *(p. 24)*

manifest functions *(p. 20)*

means of production *(p. 14)*

microlevel analysis *(p. 25)*

perspective *(p. 19)*

positivism *(p. 10)*

postmodern perspectives *(p. 26)*

power elite *(p. 22)*

proletariat *(p. 14)*

social Darwinism *(p. 12)*

social facts *(p. 13)*

social solidarity *(p. 20)*

societal consensus *(p. 20)*

society *(p. 4)*

sociological imagination *(p. 6)*

sociology *(p. 4)*

symbol *(p. 25)*

symbolic interactionist perspectives *(p. 25)*

theory *(p. 19)*

urbanization *(p. 10)*

Key Terms Quiz

Review of Key Terms – Fill In the Blanks

1. A _____ is a set of logically interrelated statements that attempts to describe, explain, and predict events.

2. _____ is the systematic study of human society and social interaction.

3. _____ _____ are intended functions that are recognized by the participants in a social unit.

4. _____ _____ are based on the assumption that society is a stable, orderly system.

5. _____ is a condition in which social control becomes ineffective as a result of the loss of shared values and a sense of purpose in society.

6. _____ _____ is a relationship in which the lives of all people are closely intertwined and any one nation's problems are part of a larger global problem.

7. _____ are those who own and control the means of production.

8. _____ _____ are the unintended functions that are hidden and remain unacknowledged by participants.

9. _____ _____ is the struggle between the capitalist and working classes.

10. _____ _____ _____ is a term for tools, land, factories, and money that form the economic basis of a society.

11. _____ _____ is a small clique of top corporate, political, and military officials.

12. _____ _____ is a situation in which the majority shares a common set of values, beliefs, and behavioural expectations.

13. _____ is a belief that the world can be best understood through scientific inquiry.

14. A _____ is an overall approach or viewpoint on some subject matter.

15. _____ _____ are patterned ways of acting, thinking, and feeling that exist outside of any one individual but that exert social control over each person.

16. _____ is a large social grouping that shares the same geographical territory and is subject to the same political authority and dominant cultural expectations.

17. A _____ is anything that meaningfully represents something else.

18. _____ _____ _____ are approaches based on the belief that society is the sum of the interactions of individuals and groups.

19. The _____ _____ is the ability to see the relationship between individual experiences and the larger society.

20. _____ _____ focuses on small groups rather than large-scale structures.

21. _____ are the undesirable consequences of any element of a society.

22. _____ is a feeling of powerlessness and estrangement from other people and from oneself.

23. _____ is the process by which an increasing proportion of a population lives in cities.

24. _____ _____ are approaches based on the belief that groups are engaged in a continuous power struggle for control of scarce resources.

25. _____ _____ refers to beliefs that guide ordinary conduct in everyday life.

26. _____ is the process by which societies are transformed from dependence on agriculture and handmade products to an emphasis on manufacturing and related industries.

27. _____ are those who sell their labour because they have no other means to earn a livelihood.

28. _____ _____ examines whole societies, large-scale social structures, and social systems.

29. _____ _____ is the state of having shared beliefs and values among members of a social group, along with intense and frequent interaction among group members.

30. _____ _____ claim that existing theories have been unsuccessful in explaining social life in contemporary societies that are characterized by postindustrialism, consumerism, and global communications.

31. _____ _____ focus on the significance of gender in understanding and explaining inequalities that exist between men and women in the household, in the paid labour force, and in the realms of politics, law, and culture.

32. _____ _____ is the belief that those species of animals (including human beings) best adapted to their environment survive and prosper, whereas those poorly adapted die out.

Key People

Auguste Comte *(p. 10)*

Emile Durkheim *(p. 13)*

Harriet Martineau *(p. 11)*

Karl Marx *(p. 14)*

George Herbert Mead *(p. 15)*

Robert K. Merton *(p. 20)*

C. Wright Mills *(p. 6)*

Talcott Parsons *(p. 20)*

Georg Simmel *(p. 16)*

Dorothy Smith *(p. 23)*

Herbert Spencer *(p. 12)*

Max Weber *(p. 15)*

Key People Quiz

Review of Key People – Matching Quiz 1

1. _____ Set forth the idea that societies are built on social facts.
2. _____ Described sociological reasoning as the sociological imagination.
3. _____ Distinguished between manifest and latent functions of social institutions.
4. _____ Translated Comte's work and explored the status of women, children, and "sufferers."
5. _____ A functionalist who claimed that all societies must make provisions for meeting social needs in order to survive.
6. _____ Believed that history is a continuous clash between conflicting ideas and forces.
7. _____ Coined the term "sociology" to describe a new science that would engage in the study of society.

a. Auguste Comte
b. Emile Durkheim
c. Harriet Martineau
d. Karl Marx
e. Robert K. Merton
f. C. Wright Mills
g. Talcott Parsons

Review of Key People − Matching Quiz 2

1. _____ Evaluated the role of the Protestant Reformation in producing a social climate in which capitalism could exist and flourish.
2. _____ Viewed society as a web of patterned interactions among people.
3. _____ Used an evolutionary perspective to explain social order and change based on the notion of "survival of the fittest."
4. _____ Argued that sociological methods, concepts, and analyses were products of the "male social universe."
5. _____ Is considered to be the founder of the symbolic interactionist perspective.

a. Georg Simmel
b. Dorothy Smith
c. Herbert Spencer
d. Max Weber
e. George H. Mead

Learning Objectives

After reading Chapter 1, the student should be able to:

1. define sociology and identify some of the benefits of studying sociology (pp. 4−6).
2. explain what C. Wright Mills meant by "sociological imagination" (pp. 6−8).
3. be able to trace the origins of sociological thinking to the Age of Enlightenment (pp. 8−10).
4. discuss industrialization and urbanization as factors that contributed to the development of sociological thinking (pp. 9−10).
5. identify Auguste Comte, Harriet Martineau, and Herbert Spencer, and explain their unique contributions to sociology (pp. 10−13).
6. explain how Durkheim's notions of "social facts" and "anomie" contribute to our understanding of society (pp. 13−14).
7. be able to outline Karl Marx's perspectives on society and social conflict (pp. 14−15).
8. explain what Max Weber meant by "value free" and "verstehen" (p. 15).
9. describe Simmel's view of society as a web of patterned interactions (p. 16).
10. describe the origins of sociology in North America and discuss the role of women in the early department of sociology and social work (pp. 16−18).
11. state the major assumptions of functionalist perspectives and identify the major contributors to functional approaches (pp. 20−22).
12. distinguish between manifest functions, latent functions, and dysfunctions (p. 20).
13. state the major assumptions of conflict perspectives and identify the key contributors (pp. 22−23).
14. describe the views of Max Weber, Ralf Dahrendorf, and C. Wright Mills on power and who holds it (p. 22).

15. identify the major assumptions of feminist perspectives (pp. 23–24).

16. understand how feminist perspectives can be used to explain suicide (p. 24).

17. distinguish between microlevel and macrolevel analyses and state which level of analysis is utilized by the interactionist perspective (pp. 24–25).

18. state the key assumptions of the symbolic interactionist perspectives and note how they can be applied to suicide (pp. 24–26).

19. describe the key assumptions of postmodern perspectives and be able to apply them to suicide (pp. 26–27).

20. note how developing your sociological imagination can lead to a career in sociology (pp. 27–29).

Unit Mastery Quizzes

Unit Mastery – Multiple Choice

1. Who translated and condensed Auguste Comte's work to make it more accessible to a wide variety of scholars?
   a. Emile Durkheim
   b. Harriet Martineau
   c. Herbert Spencer
   d. Jane Addams

2. Which of the following statements best illustrates suicide as a public issue?
   a. Suicide is an isolated act that can be understood only by studying individual personalities.
   b. Suicide is related to the issue of cohesiveness (or lack of cohesiveness) in a society.
   c. Suicide is best understood from the perspective of inherited tendencies.
   d. all of the above.

3. The development of the factory system, an emphasis on consuming, and the existence of social problems such as inadequate housing and crowding best characterizes which of the following processes?
   a. anomie
   b. socialism
   c. urbanization
   d. social Darwinism

4. Who claimed that society needed change because the majority of people are oppressed by a few wealthy capitalists?
   a. Karl Marx
   b. Emile Durkheim
   c. Georg Simmel
   d. Herbert Spencer

5. Which of the following is NOT a key reason why we study sociology?
    a. Sociology enables us to see how acts such as suicide are personal problems.
    b. Sociology helps us gain a better understanding of ourselves.
    c. Sociology helps us gain a better understanding of our social world.
    d. Sociology enables us to see how behaviour is largely shaped by the groups to which we belong.

6. Symbolic interactionist perspectives focus on:
    a. macrolevel analyses.
    b. class conflict.
    c. social facts.
    d. shared meanings.

7. Conflict perspectives examine all of the following EXCEPT:
    a. exploitation.
    b. racial oppression.
    c. consensus.
    d. patriarchy.

8. The origins of sociological thinking as we know it today can be traced to:
    a. the scientific revolution of the late seventeenth and mid-eighteenth centuries.
    b. the Age of Enlightenment.
    c. a and b above.
    d. none of the above.

9. C. Wright Mills used the term "sociological imagination" to refer to:
    a. distorting subjective biases.
    b. knowledge that guides ordinary conduct in everyday life.
    c. a relationship in which the lives of all people are closely intertwined and any one nation's problems are part of a larger global problem.
    d. the ability to see the relationship between individual experiences and the larger society.

10. A conflict approach to sexual assault would argue that:
    a. high rates of sexual assault result from learned behaviour that encourages or condones it.
    b. high rates of sexual assault result from class, race, and/or gender oppression.
    c. high rates of sexual assault result from disorganization in society.
    d. high rates of sexual assault result from the erosion of social institutions.

11. Which of the following statements is FALSE?
    a. Feminism is a single, unified approach for studying the significance of gender for explaining inequalities.
    b. Functionalists assume that a stable social system is characterized by societal consensus.
    c. According to the symbolic interactionist perspectives, society is the sum of the interactions of individuals and groups.
    d. Postmodernists claim that existing theories are unsuccessful in explaining social life in contemporary societies characterized by postindustrialization.

12. Max Weber's notion of "value free" sociology is evident in all of the following statements EXCEPT:
    a. research should be conducted in a scientific manner.
    b. research should exclude the investigator's own personal values.
    c. studies should be conducted on the basis of economic motives.
    d. attempts should be made to see the world as others see it.

13. Postmodern (or postindustrial) societies are characterized by:
    a. an information explosion.
    b. the rise of a consumer society.
    c. the emergence of a global village.
    d. all of the above.

14. Sociology thrived in Canada and the United States in the 1900s largely as a result of:
    a. the intellectual climate.
    b. a lack of social change.
    c. political stability.
    d. all of the above.

15. According to Emile Durkheim, a breakdown in traditional values and authority patterns will result in:
    a. patriarchy.
    b. group consciousness.
    c. societal consensus.
    d. anomie.

16. _____ perspectives assume that society is a stable system characterized by common values and beliefs.
    a. Conflict
    b. Functionalist
    c. Interactionist
    d. Feminist

17. Which of the following perspectives generally utilizes a macrolevel of analysis?
    a. functionalist
    b. conflict
    c. interactionist
    d. functionalist and conflict

18. Which perspective claims that how people define a situation becomes the foundation for how they behave?
    a. functionalist
    b. conflict
    c. interactionist
    d. feminist

19. Ralf Dahrendorf (1959) observed that conflict is inherent in all authority relationships and concluded that:
    a. power is the critical variable in explaining human behaviour.
    b. employers and employees hold similar beliefs and values.
    c. early socialization is largely ineffective.
    d. gender roles are socially created.

20. The transmission of knowledge and skills from one generation to the next is an example of a:
    a. dysfunction of education.
    b. manifest function of education.
    c. latent function of education.
    d. symbolic function of education.

Unit Mastery – True or False

1. Many commonsense notions are actually myths (p. 4).
    TRUE or FALSE

2. Karl Marx believed that societies were held together by strong traditions and shared moral beliefs (pp. 14–15).
    TRUE or FALSE

3. Herbert Spencer used an evolutionary perspective to explain social order and social change (pp. 12–13).
    TRUE or FALSE

4. According to symbolic interactionist perspectives, groups in society are engaged in a continuous power struggle for control of scarce resources (pp. 24–25).
    TRUE or FALSE

5. Feminist sociology incorporates both microlevel and macrolevel analysis in studying the experiences of women (p. 23).
    TRUE or FALSE

6. A symbol is anything that meaningfully represents something else (p. 25).
    TRUE or FALSE

7. Georg Simmel examined how social interactions vary as a function of group size (p. 16).
    TRUE or FALSE

8. All feminist approaches share the belief that women and men are equal (p. 24).
    TRUE or FALSE

9. Conflict perspectives assume that society is a stable, orderly system (p. 22).
    TRUE or FALSE

10. A perspective is a set of logically interrelated statements that attempt to describe, explain, and predict social events (p. 19).
    TRUE or FALSE

Unit Mastery − Fill In the Blanks

1. _____ helps us gain a better understanding of ourselves and our social world (p. 4).

2. A _____ of education can be the perpetuation of gender, racial, and class inequalities (p. 20).

3. According to _____ theorists, North American teenagers are confronted with a capitalist economy predicated on consumption and the need to achieve high levels of economic success (p. 23).

4. Mills believed that the most important decisions in society are made behind the scenes by the _____ _____ (p. 22).

5. Weber recognized the importance of economic conditions in producing inequality and conflict but added _____ and _____ as other sources of inequality (p. 22).

6. _____ perspectives assume that gender roles are socially created, rather than determined by one's biological inheritance (p. 24).

7. From a functionalist perspective, society is a stable system characterized by _____ _____ whereby the majority of members share a common set of values, beliefs, and behavioural expectations (p. 20).

8. _____ _____ are private problems of individuals and the networks of people with whom they associate regularly (p. 6).

9. Sociologist C. Wright Mills (1959) described sociological reasoning as the _____ _____ or the ability to see the relationship between individual experiences and the larger society (p. 6).

10. A _____ analysis examines whole societies, large-scale social structures, and social systems instead of looking at important social dynamics in individuals' lives (p. 24).

Unit Mastery − Matching Quiz 1

Match the concept with the appropriate theoretical perspective:

1. _____ functionalist perspective   a. social inequality
2. _____ conflict perspective   b. societal consensus
3. _____ symbolic interactionist perspective c. subjective reality
4. _____ postmodern perspective   d. patriarchy
5. _____ feminist perspective   e. global communications

Unit Mastery – Matching Quiz 2

Match the theorists to their corresponding theoretical perspectives:

1. _____ functionalist perspective
2. _____ conflict perspective
3. _____ interactionist perspective
4. _____ feminist perspective

a. Talcott Parsons and Robert Merton
b. Max Weber and C. Wright Mills
c. George Herbert Mead
d. Dorothy Smith

Unit Mastery – Matching Quiz 3

Match the concept with its originator:

1. _____ C. Wright Mills
2. _____ Emile Durkheim
3. _____ Karl Marx
4. _____ Robert K. Merton
5. _____ Auguste Comte

a. alienation
b. social fact
c. sociological imagination
d. manifest function
e. sociology

Unit Mastery – Matching Quiz 4

Match the theoretical perspective with its application to suicide:

1. _____ Higher rates of attempted suicide by young women may be an expression of their sense of powerlessness in a male-dominated society.
2. _____ There is a great deal of variation among different cultures around the world regarding the meaning of suicide.
3. _____ Suicide rates are a reflection of the degree of social solidarity in a society.
4. _____ Information technologies such as computers may create a world where people commit suicide because they feel only tenuously involved in the collective life and interpersonal relations.
5. _____ In North America, females are more likely to attempt suicide, possibly as the result of social-structural pressures on women.

a. functionalist perspective
b. conflict perspective
c. interactionist perspective
d. feminist perspective
e. postmodern perspective

Solutions

Key Terms Quiz

Review of Key Terms – Fill In the Blanks

1. theory
2. Sociology
3. Manifest functions
4. Functionalist perspectives
5. Anomie
6. Global interdependence
7. Bourgeoisie
8. Latent functions
9. Class conflict
10. Means of production
11. Power elite
12. Societal consensus
13. Positivism
14. perspective
15. Social facts
16. Society
17. symbol
18. Symbolic interactionist perspectives
19. sociological imagination
20. Microlevel analysis
21. Dysfunctions
22. Alienation
23. Urbanization
24. Conflict perspectives
25. Commonsense knowledge
26. Industrialization
27. Proletariat
28. Macrolevel analysis
29. Social solidarity
30. Postmodern perspectives
31. Feminist perspectives
32. Social Darwinism

Key People Quiz

Review of Key People – Matching Quiz 1

1. B
2. F
3. E
4. C
5. G
6. D
7. A

Review of Key People – Matching Quiz 2

1. D
2. A
3. C
4. B
5. E

Unit Mastery Quizzes

Unit Mastery – Multiple Choice

1. B
2. B
3. C
4. A
5. A
6. D
7. C
8. C
9. D
10. B
11. A
12. C
13. D
14. A
15. D
16. B
17. D
18. C
19. A
20. B

Unit Mastery – True or False

1. T
2. F, Marx stressed that history is a continuous clash between conflicting ideas and forces. Marx felt that conflict was inevitable and necessary in order to produce social change and a better society.
3. T
4. F, According to symbolic interactionist perspectives, society is the sum of the interactions of individuals and groups.
5. T
6. T
7. T
8. T
9. F, Functionalist perspectives are based on the assumption that society is a stable, orderly system.
10. F, A theory is a set of logically interrelated statements; a perspective is an overall approach.

Unit Mastery – Fill In the Blanks

1. Sociology
2. dysfunction
3. conflict
4. power elite
5. power; prestige
6. Feminist
7. societal consensus
8. Personal troubles
9. sociological imagination
10. macrolevel

Unit Mastery – Matching Quiz 1

1. B
2. A
3. C
4. E
5. D

Unit Mastery – Matching Quiz 2

1. A
2. B
3. C

4. D

Unit Mastery – Matching Quiz 3

1. C
2. B
3. A
4. D
5. E

Unit Mastery – Matching Quiz 4

1. B
2. C

3. A
4. E
5. D

Sociological Research

Chapter Outline

Chapter Summary

Sociologists conduct research to gain a more accurate understanding of society and provide a factual and objective counterpoint to commonsense knowledge and ill-informed sources of information. Sociological research is based on an empirical approach that answers questions through a direct, systematic collection and analysis of data. The two most common empirical approaches are descriptive and explanatory studies. Theory and research form a continuous cycle that encompasses both deductive and inductive approaches.

The quantitative (also called deductive) research model process begins with a research topic and a review of previous research followed by the formation of hypotheses, the development of a research design, and the collection and analysis of data. In contrast, the qualitative (or inductive) research model begins with problem formation and then proceeds with a general approach rather than a highly detailed plan that may involve redefining and reconceptualizing.

Research methods are systematic techniques for conducting research that include experiments, surveys, secondary analysis of existing data, field research, and feminist research methods. Many sociologists use multiple methods in order to gain a wider scope of data and points of view. Studying human behaviour raises important ethical issues for sociologists including the need for informed consent and voluntary participation.

Key Terms

altruism *(p. 33)*

analysis *(p. 41)*

complete observation *(p. 53)*

content analysis *(p. 52)*

control group *(p. 42)*

deductive approach *(p. 37)*

dependent variable *(p. 39)*

descriptive studies *(p. 37)*

empirical approach *(p. 35)*

ethnography *(p. 55)*

experiment *(p. 42)*

experimental group *(p. 42)*

explanatory studies *(p. 37)*

field research *(p. 53)*

hypotheses *(p. 36)*

independent variable *(p. 39)*

inductive approach *(p. 38)*

interview *(p. 47)*

normative approach *(p. 35)*

objective *(p. 36)*

operational definition *(pp. 39–40)*

participant observation *(p. 54)*

population *(p. 47)*

questionnaire *(p. 47)*

random sample *(pp. 47–48)*

reactivity *(p. 46)*

reliability *(p. 40)*

replication *(p. 41)*

representative sample *(p. 47)*

research *(p. 37)*

research methods *(p. 42)*

respondent *(p. 46)*

sample *(p. 47)*

secondary analysis *(p. 50)*

survey *(p. 46)*

theory *(p. 37)*

unstructured interview *(p. 56)*

validity *(p. 40)*

variable *(p. 38)*

Key Terms Quiz

Review of Key Terms – Fill In the Blanks

1. An _____ is a data collection encounter in which an interviewer asks the respondent questions and records the answers.

2. _____ is the repetition of the investigation in substantially the same way that it originally was conducted.

3. _____ _____ is a method in which the researcher systematically observes a social process but does not take part in it.

4. A _____ is the term used for the people who are selected from the population to be studied.

5. A _____ is any concept with measurable traits or characteristics that can change from one person, time, situation, or society to another.

6. A _____ is set of logically interrelated statements that attempts to describe, explain, and predict social events.

7. _____ _____ is an explanation of an abstract concept in terms of observable features that are specific enough to measure the variable.

8. _____ are tentative statements of the relationship between two or more concepts or variables.

9. An _____ is a carefully designed situation in which the researcher studies the impact of certain variables on subjects' attitudes or behaviour.

10. A _____ _____ is the term used for the subjects who are not exposed to the independent variable.

11. _____ is a term used for persons about whom we want to be able to draw conclusions.

12. _____ _____ is a term used in research for findings that are based on the assumption that knowledge is best gained by direct, systematic observation.

13. A _____ is a research method in which a number of respondents are asked identical questions through a systematic questionnaire or interview.

14. _____ is when scientists try to ensure that their biases and values do not affect their research.

15. _____ is the process through which data are organized so that comparisons can be made and conclusions drawn.

16. A _____ is a printed research instrument containing a series of items to which subjects respond.

17. _____ is the extent to which a study or research instrument yields consistent results.

18. _____ is the extent to which a study or research instrument accurately measures what it is supposed to measure.

19. The _____ _____ uses religion, tradition, or authority to answer important questions.

20. The _____ _____ begins with a theory and uses research to test the theory.

21. A _____ _____ is a selection from a larger population that has the essential characteristics of the total population.

22. An _____ _____ is research that attempts to explain relationships and provides information on why certain events do or do not occur.

23. An _____ _____ contains the subjects who are exposed to an independent variable.

24. _____ are persons who provide data for analysis through interviews or questionnaires.

25. A _____ _____ is a variable that is assumed to depend on or be caused by the independent variable(s).

26. _____ _____ attempt to describe social reality or provide facts about some group, practice, or event.

27. An _____ _____ is a variable presumed to cause or determine a dependent variable.

28. An _____ _____ is an extended, open-ended interaction between an interviewer and interviewee.

29. _____ _____ is a term used for when researchers collect information or data (facts or evidence) and then generate theories from the analysis of that data.

30. _____ _____ is a method in which researchers use existing material and analyze data originally collected by others.

31. A _____ _____ _____ is a group of people chosen for research by chance: every member of an entire population has the same chance of being selected.

32. An _____ is a detailed study of the life and activities of a group of people by researchers who may live that group over a period of years.

33. _____ _____ is a method in which researchers collect systematic observations while being part of the activities of the group they are studying.

34. _____ is the tendency of participants to change their behaviour in response to the presence of the researcher or to the fact that they know they are being studied.

35. _____ is behaviour intended to help others and done without any expectation of personal benefit.

36. _____ _____ is the study of social life in its natural setting: observing and interviewing people where they live, work, and play.

37. _____ is the process of systematically collecting information for the purposes of testing an existing theory or generating a new one.

38. _____ _____ are specific strategies or techniques for conducting research.

39. _____ _____ is the systematic examination of cultural artifacts or various forms of communication to extract thematic data and draw conclusions about social life.

Key People

Margrit Eichler *(p. 57)*

Laud Humphreys *(p. 59)*

David Karp and William Yoels *(p. 53)*

Bibb Latané and John Darley *(p. 43)*

Russel Ogden *(p. 60)*

Pitirim Sorokin *(p. 50)*

Richard Titmuss *(p. 48)*

Louis Zurcher *(p. 54)*

Key People Quiz

Review of Key People – Matching Quiz

1. _____ Has identified several limitations in research that relate to gender, including approaching issues from only a male perspective and viewing women only in terms of how they relate to men.

2. _____ Surveyed blood donors to try to understand the reasons for this form of altruism.

3. _____ Studied homosexual behaviour in public washrooms.

4. _____ Studied altruism by examining good neighbour recommendation letters and biographical information on saints.

5. _____ Studied helping behaviour and how communities recover following natural disasters (e.g., tornadoes).

6. _____ Refused to testify in the possible assisted suicide of an AIDS victim on grounds of confidentiality.

7. _____ Conducted a complete observation study on student participation in university classrooms.

8. _____ Hypothesized that the presence of others would inhibit a helping response when people were faced with an emergency.

a. Margrit Eichler
b. Laud Humphreys
c. David Karp and William Yoels
d. Bibb Latané and John Darley
e. Russel Ogden
f. Pitirim Sorokin
g. Richard Titmuss
h. Louis Zurcher

Learning Objectives

After reading Chapter 2, the student should be able to:

1. list and describe the five ways of knowing the world (pp. 34–35).

2. compare normative and empirical approaches to examining social issues (p. 35).

3. describe descriptive and explanatory studies and indicate how researchers decide which one to use (p. 37).

4. list the four main steps in the deductive and inductive approaches (pp. 37–38).

5. be able to describe each step in the quantitative research model (pp. 38–41).

6. indicate the relationship between independent and dependent variables (p. 39).

7. explain why reliability and validity are important considerations in sociological research (pp. 40–41).

8. identify the main steps in the qualitative research model and be familiar with the unique features of this model research (pp. 41–42).

9. contrast experimental and control groups and explain why control groups are necessary in experiments (pp. 42–43).

10. be able to state the major independent and dependent variables in Latané and Darley's experiment on helping in an emergency situation. Also describe the key findings (pp. 43–46).

11. outline the major strengths and weaknesses of experimental research methods (p. 46).

12. describe the major types of surveys (p. 47).

13. distinguish between a representative sample and a random sample (p. 47).

14. indicate the major strengths and weaknesses of survey research (p. 50).

15. define secondary analysis, and note some of the sources of secondary data (pp. 50–53).

16. state the major strengths and weaknesses of secondary analysis of existing data (p. 54).

17. describe the major methods of field research and indicate when researchers are most likely to utilize each of them (pp. 53–57).

18. note the key features of feminist research methods (pp. 57–58).

19. be able to distinguish between social research methods (i.e., experiments, surveys, secondary data analyses, and field research) (see chart, p. 58).

20. describe the major ethical concerns in sociological research and note which ethical issues are raised by Humphreys and Ogden's research (pp. 59–61).

Unit Mastery Quizzes

Unit Mastery – Multiple Choice

1. _____ is a means through which we come to know about the world.
   a. Personal experience
   b. Tradition
   c. Authority
   d. all of the above

2. Which of the following indicates a correct ordering of steps in the quantitative research model?
   a. select and define the research problem, develop the research design, formulate hypotheses, collect the data, analyze the data, review the literature.
   b. select and define the research problem, develop the research design, collect the data, analyze the data, review the literature, generate hypotheses.
   c. select and define the research problem, review the literature, formulate the hypotheses, develop the research design, collect the data, analyze the data, draw conclusions
   d. select and define the research problem, collect the data, analyze the data, develop the research design, formulate hypotheses, draw conclusions

3. In Latané and Darley's experiment on helping in emergency situations, the main dependent variable was:
   a. participant's medical background.
   b. group size.
   c. number of bystanders.
   d. time to help.

4. In which approach to sociological research do you formulate hypotheses near the beginning of the process?
   a. inclusive
   b. qualitative
   c. inductive
   d. deductive

5. Science uses this approach when it relies on direct, systematic observation.
   a. normative
   b. empirical
   c. inductive
   d. deductive

6. What type of study is likely to report on census data or try to determine the number of people who recently contemplated suicide?
   a. descriptive
   b. explanatory
   c. experimental
   d. unstructured

7. A recurring issue in studies that analyze the relationship between religious beliefs and suicide is whether "church membership" is an accurate indicator of a person's religious beliefs. This example demonstrates which problem in research?
   a. objectivity
   b. sampling errors
   c. validity
   d. reliability

8. Which of the following is NOT a limitation of experiments?
   a. They are artificial.
   b. Participants may change their behaviour as a result of being studied.
   c. Researchers have control over the environment.
   d. Experimenters frequently rely on volunteers or captive audiences such as students.

9. An advantage of survey research is:
   a. it is useful in describing the characteristics of a large population without having to interview each person in the population.
   b. it enables the researcher to search for causes and effects.
   c. people's opinions on issues seldom take the form of a standard response.
   d. all of the above.

10. Observation, case studies, and unstructured interviews are techniques used to obtain data using which form of research?
    a. experimental
    b. field
    c. survey
    d. secondary data analysis

11. Which variable is assumed to be the cause of another one?
    a. control
    b. independent
    c. dependent
    d. intervening

12. Which of the following statements about sampling is TRUE?
    a. When using a simple random sample, every member of an entire population being studied has an equal chance of being selected.
    b. A representative sample includes the entire population we are interested in.
    c. A sample consists of those persons about whom we want to be able to draw conclusions.
    d. Sampling is a technique used to assign participants to conditions in experiments.

13. Sorokin examined altruism through good neighbour recommendation letters and biographies of saints. This research involved which method?
    a. field experiment
    b. survey
    c. experimental
    d. secondary data analysis

14. What type of survey technique involves an interviewer who asks respondents questions and records their answers?
    a. questionnaire
    b. self-administered survey
    c. interview
    d. unobtrusive

15. If you were interested in finding out how much violence is contained in children's television shows, you would most likely adopt which method of research?
    a. experiment
    b. survey
    c. secondary analysis
    d. ethnography

16. Which of the following statements concerning feminist research methods is TRUE?
    a. Feminist research tries to provide explanations of women's lives that are useful for improving their situations.
    b. Feminist research involves completely different methods of data collection than those used by sociologists.
    c. The survey approach is termed the "feminist methodology."
    d. Feminist research is centred on showing how males dominate society.

17. Secondary data analysis may include all of the following EXCEPT:
    a. Obtaining raw data collected by other researchers and undertaking a statistical analysis of the data.
    b. An analysis of existing statistical information.
    c. An examination of love letters and poetry between newlywed couples.
    d. Collecting observations while being part of the activities of the group being studied.

18. Which research method has a high degree of control but is artificial by nature and frequently raises ethical issues?
    a. experiments
    b. survey research
    c. secondary analysis
    d. field research

19. Which of the following examples would be considered unethical in sociological research?
    a. The researcher was careful not to reveal information that would embarrass the participants in the study.
    b. Participants in an experiment consisted of students who were in the study as part of their course requirements.
    c. Students filling out teacher evaluations were told not to put their names or any identifying information on the forms they filled out.
    d. Participants in an experiment were told that the exercise they were about to perform had a slight risk of physical injury.

20. In an experiment, the group of people who participate in the study but are not exposed to the independent variable represent:
    a. the experimental group.
    b. the independent condition.
    c. the dependent condition.
    d. the control group.

Unit Mastery − True or False

1. The normative approach is based on strong beliefs about what is right and wrong and what ought to be in society (p. 35).
    TRUE or FALSE

2. In the deductive approach, the researcher collects information and then generates theories from the analysis of that data (p. 37).
    TRUE or FALSE

3. The independent variable is caused by the dependent one (p. 39).
    TRUE or FALSE

4. A population consists of the people about whom we wish to draw conclusions (p. 47).
    TRUE or FALSE

5. Reliability concerns the extent to which an instrument measures what it is supposed to (p. 40).
    TRUE or FALSE

6. Drawing conclusions and reporting on the findings is the last stage in the research process (p. 41).
    TRUE or FALSE

7. The major disadvantage of interviews is cost and time (p. 47).
    TRUE or FALSE

8. Field researchers use methods that generate quantitative data (p. 53).
    TRUE or FALSE

9. A respondent is anonymous if the research is able to identify a given person's responses but essentially promises not to do so (p. 59).
    TRUE or FALSE

10. Most participant observation research takes the form of a case study (p. 55).
    TRUE or FALSE

Unit Mastery − Fill In the Blanks

1. In _____ observations, the researcher systematically observers a social process but does not take part in it (p. 53).

2. Survey research uses _____ interviews in which the interviewers asks questions from a standardized questionnaire (p. 46).

3. The _____ _____ is based on the assumption that knowledge is best gained by direct, systematic observation (p. 35).

4. The theory and research cycle consists of both _____ and _____ approaches (p. 37).

5. A _____ is any concept with measurable traits or characteristics that can vary from one person, time, situation, or society to another (p. 38).

6. _____ is the process of systematically collecting information for the purposes of testing an existing theory or generating a new one (p. 37).

7. _____ are designed to create "real-life" situations, ideally under controlled circumstances in which the influence of different variables can be modified and measured (p. 42).

8. _____ are persons who provide data for analysis through interviews or questionnaires (p. 46).

9. Experiments have the problem of _____ , where participants change their behaviour in response to the presence of the researcher or to the fact that they know they are being studied (p. 46).

10. Researchers frequently select a _____ _____ from a larger population that has the essential characteristics of the total population (p. 47).

Unit Mastery − Matching Quiz 1

Match the research method with its appropriate form of data collection:

1. _____ questionnaire	a.	experiment
2. _____ laboratory	b.	survey
3. _____ existing statistics	c.	secondary analysis
4. _____ case study	d.	field research

Unit Mastery − Matching Quiz 2

Match the research method with its major strength:

1. _____ data often readily available, inexpensive to collect	a.	experiment
	b.	survey
2. _____ can describe features of a large population without interviewing everyone	c.	secondary analysis
	d.	field research
3. _____ opportunity to gain an insider's view, useful for studying behaviour in natural settings		
4. _____ control over research, is relatively inexpensive		

Unit Mastery – Matching Quiz 3

Match the research method with its major weakness:

1. _____ difficulty in determining accuracy of data, data may not meet researchers' goals
2. _____ problems in generalizing the results, nonprecise data measurements
3. _____ frequent reliance on volunteers, artificial by nature
4. _____ potentially forced answers, respondent dishonesty

a. experiment
b. survey
c. secondary analysis
d. field research

Solutions

Key Terms Quiz
Review of Key Terms – Fill In the Blanks

1. interview
2. Replication
3. Complete observation
4. sample
5. variable
6. theory
7. Operational definition
8. Hypotheses
9. experiment
10. control group
11. Population
12. Empirical approach
13. survey
14. Objective
15. Analysis
16. questionnaire
17. Reliability
18. Validity
19. normative approach
20. deductive approach
21. representative sample
22. explanatory study
23. experimental group
24. Respondents
25. dependent variable
26. Descriptive studies
27. independent variable
28. unstructured interview
29. Inductive approach
30. Secondary analysis
31. simple random sample
32. ethnography
33. Participant observation
34. Reactivity
35. Altruism
36. Field research
37. Research
38. Research methods
39. Content analysis

Key People Quiz
Review of Key People – Matching Quiz

1. A
2. G
3. B
4. F
5. H
6. E
7. C
8. D

Unit Mastery Quizzes
Unit Mastery – Multiple Choice

1. D
2. C
3. D
4. D
5. B
6. A
7. C
8. C
9. A
10. B
11. B
12. A
13. D
14. C
15. C
16. A
17. D
18. A
19. B
20. D

Unit Mastery – True or False

1. T
2. F, In the deductive approach, the researcher begins with a theory and uses research to test the theory.
3. F, The dependent variable (or outcome) is caused by the independent variable.
4. T
5. F, Validity is the extent to which a study or research instrument accurately measures what it is supposed to measure.
6. T
7. T
8. F, Field researchers use observations, face-to-face discussions, and participation in events to generate qualitative data.
9. F, Maintaining confidentiality means that the researcher can identify a given person's responses with that person but promises not to do so.
10. T

Unit Mastery – Fill In the Blanks

1. complete
2. structured
3. empirical approach
4. deductive; inductive
5. variable
6. Research
7. Experiments
8. Respondents
9. reactivity
10. representative sample

Unit Mastery − Matching Quiz 1

1. B
2. A
3. C
4. D

Unit Mastery − Matching Quiz 2

1. C
2. B
3. D
4. A

Unit Mastery − Matching Quiz 3

1. C
2. D
3. A
4. B

Culture

Chapter Outline

I. The Importance of Culture and Society in a Changing World

   A. The Importance of Culture

   B. Material and Nonmaterial Culture

   C. Cultural Universals

II. Components of Culture

   A. Symbols

   B. Language

   C. Values

   D. Norms

III. Technology, Cultural Change, and Diversity

   A. Cultural Change

   B. Cultural Diversity

   C. Culture Shock

   D. Ethnocentrism and Cultural Relativism

IV. A Global Popular Culture

   A. High Culture and Popular Culture

   B. Forms of Popular Culture

V. Sociological Analysis of Culture

   A. Functionalist Perspectives

   B. Conflict Perspectives

   C. Feminist Perspectives

   D. Symbolic Interactionist Perspectives

   E. Postmodern Perspectives

VI. Culture in the Future

Chapter Summary

Culture is the knowledge, language, values, customs, and material objects that are passed from person to person and from generation to generation. At the macrolevel, culture can be a stabilizing force or a source of conflict. At the microlevel, culture is essential for individual survival. Sociologists distinguish between material and nonmaterial culture. Material culture consists of the physical or tangible creations that members of a society make, use, and share. Nonmaterial culture consists of the abstract or intangible human creations of society that influence people's behaviour. According to the Sapir–Whorf hypothesis, language shapes our perception of reality. Language may create and reinforce inaccurate perceptions based on gender, race, or ethnicity. While it is assumed that high culture appeals primarily to elite audiences, popular culture appeals to members of the middle and working classes.

In Canada, diversity is reflected through race, ethnicity, age, sexual orientation, religion, occupation, and so forth. Culture shock refers to the anxiety people experience when they encounter cultures radically different from their own. Ethnocentrism, an assumption that one's own culture is superior to others, is counterbalanced by cultural relativism, the belief that behaviours and customs of a society must be examined within the context of that culture. As we look toward even more diverse and global cultural patterns in the future, it is important to keep our sociological imaginations actively engaged.

Key Terms

counterculture *(p. 84)*
cultural imperialism *(p. 87)*
cultural lag *(p. 79)*
cultural relativism *(p. 86)*
cultural universals *(p. 70)*
culture *(p. 66)*
culture shock *(p. 85)*
diffusion *(p. 80)*
discovery *(p. 80)*
ethnocentrism *(p. 86)*
folkways *(p. 78)*
ideal culture *(p. 78)*
invention *(p. 80)*
language *(p. 72)*
laws *(p. 79)*

material culture *(p. 69)*
mores *(p. 79)*
nonmaterial culture *(p. 69)*
norms *(p. 78)*
popular culture *(p. 86)*
real culture *(p. 78)*
sanctions *(p. 78)*
Sapir–Whorf hypothesis *(p. 73)*
subculture *(p. 83)*
symbol *(p. 71)*
taboos *(p. 79)*
technology *(p. 69)*
values *(p. 77)*
value contradictions *(p. 77)*

Key Terms Quiz

Review of Key Terms – Fill In the Blanks

1. _____ are formal, standardized norms that have been enacted by legislatures and are enforced by formal sanctions.

2. _____ are established rules of behaviour or standards of conduct.

3. _____ are strongly held norms with moral and ethical connotations that may not be violated without serious consequences in a particular culture.

4. _____ are rewards for appropriate behaviour or penalties for inappropriate acts.

5. _____ are mores so strong that their violation is considered extremely offensive and even unmentionable.

6. _____ are informal norms or everyday customs that may be violated without serious consequences.

7. _____ _____ is the values and standards of behaviour that people in a society profess to hold.

8. _____ _____ consists of activities, products, and services that are assumed to appeal primarily to members of the middle and working classes.

9. _____ _____ consists of the abstract or intangible human creations of society that influence people's behaviour.

10. _____ _____ are customs and practices that occur across all societies.

11. _____ is the knowledge, language, values, customs, and material objects that are passed from person to person and from one generation to the next in a human group or society.

12. _____ is the knowledge, techniques, and tools that make it possible for people to transform resources into usable forms, and the knowledge and skills required to use them after they are developed.

13. _____ _____ consists of the physical or tangible creations that members of a society make, use, and share.

14. _____ is a group that strongly rejects dominant societal values and norms and seeks alternative lifestyles.

15. _____ _____ is a gap between the technical development of a society and its moral and legal institutions.

16. _____ _____ is the belief that the behaviours and customs of any culture must be viewed and analyzed by the culture's own standards.

17. _____ _____ is the disorientation that people feel when they encounter cultures radically different from their own.

18. _____ is the tendency to regard one's own culture and group as the standard, and thus superior, whereas all other groups are seen as inferior.

19. _____ _____ is the extensive infusion of one nation's culture into other nations.

20. _____ is the transmission of cultural items or social practices from one group or society to another.

21. _____ is the process of learning about something previously unknown or unrecognized.

22. _____ is the process of reshaping existing cultural items into a new form.

23. _____ is a set of symbols that express ideas and enable people to think and communicate with one another.

24. _____ are collective ideas about what is right or wrong, good or bad, and desirable or undesirable in a particular culture.

25. _____ is a group of people who share a distinctive set of cultural beliefs and behaviours that differ in some significant way from that of the larger society.

26. _____ _____ are values that conflict with one another or are mutually exclusive.

27. _____ _____ is the values and standards of behaviour that people actually follow.

28. _____ _____ is a claim that language shapes the view of reality of its speakers.

29. A _____ is anything that meaningfully represents something else.

Key People

Jean Baudrillard *(p. 91)*

Pierre Bourdieu *(p. 86)*

Napoleon Chagnon *(p. 85)*

Stephen M. Fjellman *(p. 91)*

Marvin Harris *(p. 86)*

K. Sue Jewell *(p. 90)*

Bronislaw Malinowski *(p. 89)*

William F. Ogburn *(p. 79)*

Edward Sapir and Benjamin Whorf *(p. 73)*

Key People Quiz

Review of Key People – Matching Quiz 1

1. _____ Studied Walt Disney World from a functional perspective and found that amusement parks allow people to forget the outside world, including how threatening it can be.

2. _____ Used cultural relativism to explain why cattle are not eaten in India despite widespread hunger and malnutrition.

3. _____ This sociologist's cultural capital theory views high culture as a device used by the dominant class to exclude subordinate classes.

4. _____ Experienced culture shock when he first encountered the Yanomamö, a tribe in South America.

5. _____ Contends that the world of culture today is based on simulation, not reality.

a. Pierre Bourdieu
b. Napoleon Chagnon
c. Stephen M. Fjellman
d. Marvin Harris
e. Jean Baudrillard

Review of Key People − Matching Quiz 2

1. _____ Used the term "cultural lag" to refer to the failure of nonmaterial culture to keep pace with the material culture.

2. _____ Suggested that culture helps people meet their biological, instrumental, and integral needs.

3. _____ Linked images found in popular culture to negative stereotypes of Black women.

4. _____ Suggested that language shapes our perceptions of reality.

a. K. Sue Jewell
b. Bronislaw Malinowski
c. William F. Ogburn
d. Edward Sapir and Benjamin Whorf

Learning Objectives

After reading Chapter 3, the student should be able to:

1. explain what culture is and describe the importance of culture in determining how people think and act on a daily basis (pp. 66−68).

2. define and distinguish between material and nonmaterial culture (pp. 69−70).

3. be able to list and describe the four main components of culture (pp. 71−79).

4. outline the importance of language for determining social reality and explain what is meant by the Sapir−Whorf hypothesis (pp. 72−73).

5. describe the relationship between language and gender, and note how language is implicated in negative racial and ethnic stereotypes (pp. 73−75).

6. understand how language diversity affects Canadian culture (pp. 75−77).

7. list and briefly explain the core values in Canadian society (p. 77).

8. contrast ideal and real culture and give examples of each (p. 78).

9. state the definition of norms and distinguish between folkways, mores, and laws (pp. 78−79).

10. distinguish between discovery, invention, and diffusion as means of cultural change, and explain why the rate of cultural change is uneven (p. 80).

11. note some of the costly mistakes advertisers have made when attempting to sell a product in a foreign culture (see Box 3.2, p. 81).

12. describe subcultures and countercultures and give examples of each (pp. 83−85).

13. state the definitions for culture shock, ethnocentrism, and cultural relativism, and explain the relationship between these three concepts (pp. 85−86).

14. distinguish between high culture and popular culture (pp. 86−87).

15. note the main forms of popular culture (pp. 87−88).

16. describe how the functionalist perspective views culture (p. 89).

17. understand the assumptions of a conflict perspective on culture (pp. 89−90).

18. explain how the symbolic interactionist view of culture differs from the structural functional and conflict perspectives (pp. 90–91).

19. explain what postmodernist Baudrillard meant by the contention that the world of culture today is based on simulation, not reality (p. 91).

20. outline the predictions for cultural trends in the future (p. 92).

Unit Mastery Quizzes

Unit Mastery – Multiple Choice

1. The relationship between language and gender is evident in the fact that:
   a. the English language ignores women through its use of the masculine form to refer to humans in general.
   b. when referring to occupations, pronouns tend to show the gender of the person we expect to hold that occupation.
   c. words are more likely to have positive connotations when relating to male power, prestige, and leadership.
   d. all of the above examples show a relationship between language and gender.

2. Some languages do not contain past, present, or future tenses for time, suggesting that language may affect how we experience reality. This phenomenon is known as:
   a. ethnography.
   b. the Sapir–Whorf hypothesis.
   c. diffusion of reality.
   d. nonmaterial culture.

3. The notions of equality and fairness in a democratic society represent:
   a. core Canadian values.
   b. positive sanctions.
   c. popular culture in Canada.
   d. ethnocentrism.

4. Thinking of yourself as a "good citizen" despite regularly driving over the speed limit demonstrates the distinction between:
   a. folkways and mores.
   b. ideal versus real culture.
   c. popular versus high culture.
   d. formal and informal norms.

5. Culture includes all of the following components EXCEPT:
   a. values.
   b. symbols.
   c. language.
   d. diversity.

6. Which of the following statements concerning culture is FALSE?
    a. Culture is made up of ideas, behaviour, and material possessions.
    b. Culture can generate discord, conflict, and even violence.
    c. Culture exists independent of society.
    d. Culture can at times be a stabilizing force that provides a sense of continuity.

7. Cultural change, at both material and nonmaterial levels is likely the result of:
    a. discovery.
    b. invention.
    c. diffusion.
    d. all of the above can contribute to cultural change.

8. Hutterites who live on farms in western Canada can be considered a:
    a. subculture.
    b. counterculture.
    c. xenocentrist group.
    d. population culture.

9. In 1969, the federal government passed the Official Languages Act:
    a. making French the official language of Quebec and English the official language for the remaining Canadian provinces.
    b. making French, English, and Ukrainian the official languages in Canada.
    c. making English the official language in Canada.
    d. making French and English official languages in Canada.

10. Cultural diversity:
    a. refers to the wide range of cultural differences found between and within nations.
    b. between countries may be the result of natural circumstances (such as climate and geography).
    c. between countries may be the result of social circumstances (such as level of technology and composition of the population).
    d. all of the above.

11. Rock concerts, movies, and spectator sports are characteristic of:
    a. nonmaterial culture.
    b. high culture.
    c. popular culture.
    d. ideal culture.

12. Cars, clothes, computers, and books are examples of:
    a. technology.
    b. nonmaterial culture.
    c. material culture.
    d. symbols.

13. Who claims popular culture may be the "glue" that holds society together?
    a. functionalists
    b. symbolic interactionists
    c. conflict theorists
    d. feminists

14. If a Canadian teenager who was used to roller blades and computer games woke to find him or herself among the Yanomamö tribe of South America, he or she would immediately experience:
    a. cultural relativism.
    b. subcultures.
    c. culture shock.
    d. false consciousness.

15. As we enter the future, we are likely to experience:
    a. a breakdown in the global culture that has existed for hundreds of years.
    b. an acceleration in the flow of information and expanded cultural diffusion.
    c. less reliance on the television as a window on the world.
    d. an end to cultural diversity and the emergence of a distinctly Canadian identity.

16. When MacDonald's ventured into China, they paraded Ronald MacDonald around, not realizing that to the Chinese, a clown symbolizes death. This example illustrates:
    a. invention.
    b. cultural shock.
    c. cultural lag.
    d. ethnocentrism.

17. Which perspective claims that values and norms help create and sustain the privileged position of the powerful in society while excluding others?
    a. functionalist
    b. conflict
    c. symbolic interactionist
    d. feminist

18. According to _____ theory, people continually negotiate their social realities.
    a. functionalist
    b. conflict
    c. symbolic interactionist
    d. feminist

19. Which perspective focuses on the needs of society and the fact that stability is essential for society's continued survival?
    a. functionalist
    b. conflict
    c. symbolic interactionist
    d. feminist

20. Not giving up your seat to an elderly or disabled person while riding on a city bus violates a:
    a. folkway.
    b. more.
    c. taboo.
    d. value.

Unit Mastery – True or False

1. A central component of nonmaterial culture is beliefs (p. 69).
   TRUE or FALSE

2. Recreational activities, forms of appearance such as hairstyles, and social institutions are considered cultural universals because they exist in all societies (p. 70).
   TRUE or FALSE

3. The flower children of the 1960s and the drug enthusiasts of the 1970s are considered subcultures because they opposed the larger society (p. 84).
   TRUE or FALSE

4. The belief that the products, styles, or ideas of another society are better than one's own culture is known as ethnocentrism (p. 86).
   TRUE or FALSE

5. Culture could not exist without symbols because there would be no shared meanings among people (p. 71).
   TRUE or FALSE

6. Civil law deals with disputes among persons or groups (p. 79).
   TRUE or FALSE

7. Functionalists focus on a microlevel analysis that views society as the sum of all people's interactions (p. 89).
   TRUE or FALSE

8. Conflict perspectives are based on the assumption that social life is a continuous struggle in which members of powerful groups seek to control scarce resources (p. 89).
   TRUE or FALSE

9. Immigration contributes to cultural diversity in Canada (p. 81).
   TRUE or FALSE

10. Popular culture consists of classical music, opera, and live theatre (p. 86).
    TRUE or FALSE

Unit Mastery – Fill In the Blanks

1. _____ are collective ideas about what is right or wrong, but they do not dictate how we should behave (p. 77).

2. Language, beliefs, values, rules of behaviour, family patterns, and political systems are examples of
    _____ _____ (p. 69).

3. _____ theorists believe that much of what has been written about culture in the Western
    world is Eurocentric (p. 91).

4. _____ can create and reinforce our perceptions about race and ethnicity by transmitting
    preconceived ideas about the superiority of one category of people over another (p. 75).

5. _____ provide rules for conduct but are not considered to be essential to society's survival
    (p. 78).

6. The incest _____ prohibits sexual or marital relations between certain categories of kin (p. 79).

7. Pierre Bourdieu's (1984) _____ _____ _____ views high culture as a device
    used by the dominant class to exclude the subordinate classes (p. 86).

8. Unlike high culture, _____ _____ is assumed to be far more widespread and
    accessible to everyone (p. 87).

9. Occupational groups such as lawyers and ethnic populations such as Italian Canadians are examples
    of _____ (p. 83).

10. A _____ _____ approach highlights how people maintain and change culture
    through their interactions with others (p. 91).

Unit Mastery – Matching Quiz 1

Match each example with the corresponding type of norm:

1. _____ taboo
2. _____ folkway
3. _____ law

a. Standing up while the national anthem is playing.
b. A sexual relationship between siblings.
c. Committing first-degree murder.

Unit Mastery – Matching Quiz 2

Match each statement with the appropriate theoretical perspective:

1. _____ functionalist
2. _____ conflict
3. _____ symbolic interactionist
4. _____ postmodernist

a. Culture today is based on simulation not reality.
b. Culture meets biological and integrative needs.
c. Values are reinterpreted in every social situation.
d. Values help maintain the positions of those in power.

Solutions

Key Terms Quiz

Review of Key Terms – Fill In the Blanks

1. Laws
2. Norms
3. Mores
4. Sanctions
5. Taboos
6. Folkways
7. Ideal culture
8. Popular culture
9. Nonmaterial culture
10. Cultural universals
11. Culture
12. Technology
13. Material culture
14. Counterculture
15. Cultural lag
16. Cultural relativism
17. Culture shock
18. Ethnocentrism
19. Cultural imperialism
20. Diffusion
21. Discovery
22. Invention
23. Language
24. Values
25. Subculture
26. Value contradictions
27. Real culture
28. Sapir–Whorf hypothesis
29. symbol

Key People Quiz

Review of Key People – Matching Quiz 1

1. C
2. D
3. A
4. B
5. E

Review of Key People – Matching Quiz 2

1. C
2. B
3. A
4. D

Unit Mastery Quizzes

Unit Mastery – Multiple Choice

1. D
2. B
3. A
4. B
5. D
6. C
7. D
8. A
9. D
10. D
11. C
12. C
13. A
14. C
15. B
16. D
17. B
18. C
19. A
20. A

Unit Mastery – True or False

1. T
2. T
3. F, They constitute countercultures because the groups strongly reject dominant societal values and norms and seek alternative lifestyles.
4. F, Ethnocentrism refers to the tendency to regard one's own culture and group as the standard, and thus superior.
5. T
6. T
7. F, Symbolic interactionists engage in a microlevel analysis that views society as the sum of all people's interactions.
8. T
9. T
10. F, High culture consists of classical music, ballet, live theatre, and other activities usually patronized by elite audiences.

Unit Mastery – Fill In the Blanks

1. Values
2. nonmaterial culture
3. Postmodernist
4. Language
5. Folkways
6. taboo
7. cultural capital theory
8. popular culture
9. subcultures
10. symbolic interactionist

Unit Mastery – Matching Quiz 1

1. B
2. A
3. C

Unit Mastery – Matching Quiz 2

1. B
2. D
3. C
4. A

Socialization

Chapter Outline

Chapter Summary

Socialization is the lifelong process through which individuals acquire a self-identity and the physical, mental, and social skills needed for survival. Socialization is essential for the individual's survival, for human development, and for the survival and stability of society. People are a product of two forces: heredity and the social environment. Most sociologists agree that while biology dictates our physical makeup, the social environment largely determines how we develop and behave. Children who are isolated during their formative years fail to develop their full emotional and intellectual capacities. Social contact is essential in developing a self, or self-concept.

According to sociologists, agents of socialization—including families, schools, peer groups, and the media—teach us what we need to know in order to participate in society. Charles Horton Cooley developed the image of the looking-glass self to explain how people see themselves through the perceptions of others. George Herbert Mead linked the idea of self-concept to role-taking and to learning the rules of social interaction. While Cooley's and Mead's theories are sociologically based, the theories of Sigmund Freud, Jean Piaget, Lawrence Kohlberg, and Carol Gilligan are based in psychology. Social class, gender, and race are determining factors in the lifelong socialization process. We learn knowledge and skills for future roles through anticipatory socialization.

Resocialization—the learning new attitudes, values, and behaviours—sometimes takes place in total institutions. We must not only learn about the past but also acquire the knowledge and skills to think about the future in a practical manner.

Key Terms

agents of socialization *(p. 104)*

anticipatory socialization *(p. 115)*

ego *(p. 112)*

gender socialization *(pp. 114−115)*

generalized other *(p. 111)*

id *(p. 112)*

looking-glass self *(p. 108)*

peer group *(p. 106)*

resocialization *(p. 118)*

role-taking *(p. 109)*

self-concept *(p. 108)*

significant others *(p. 110)*

social devaluation *(p. 117)*

socialization *(p. 99)*

sociobiology *(p. 101)*

superego *(p. 113)*

total institution *(pp. 119−120)*

Key Terms Quiz

Review of Key Terms − Fill In the Blanks

1. _____ _____ is a situation wherein a person or group is considered to have less social value than other individuals or groups.

2. _____ or conscience, consists of the moral and ethical aspects of personality.

3. _____ is the rational, reality-oriented component of personality that imposes restrictions on the innate pleasure-seeking drives of the id.

4. _____ is the component of personality that includes all of the individual's basic biological drives and needs that demand immediate gratification.

5. _____ is the systematic study of how biology affects social behaviour.

6. _____ _____ is the child's awareness of the demands and expectations of the society as a whole or of the child's subculture.

7. _____ _____ is a group of people who are linked by common interests, equal social position, and (usually) similar age.

8. _____ is the lifelong process of social interaction through which individuals acquire a self-identity and the physical, mental, and social skills needed for survival in society.

9. _____ is the process by which a person mentally assumes the role of another person in order to understand the world from that person's point of view.

10. _____ _____ are those persons whose care, affection, and approval are especially desired and who are the most important in the development of the self.

11. _____ _____ is the way in which a person's sense of self is derived from the perceptions of others.

12. _____ _____ _____ are the persons, groups, or institutions that teach us what we need to know in order to participate in society.

13. _____ _____ is the aspect of socialization that contains specific messages and practices concerning the nature of being female or male in a specific group or society.

14. _____ is the process of learning a new and different set of attitudes, values, and behaviours from those in one's previous background and experience.

15. _____ is the totality of our beliefs and feelings about ourselves.

16. _____ _____ is a place where people are isolated from the rest of society for a set period of time and come under the control of the officials who run the institution.

17. _____ _____ is the process by which knowledge and skills are learned for future roles.

Key People

Charles Horton Cooley *(p. 108)*

Sigmund Freud *(p. 112)*

Carol Gilligan *(p. 114)*

Lawrence Kohlberg *(p. 113)*

George Herbert Mead *(p. 109)*

Wilbert Moore *(p. 117)*

Jean Piaget *(p. 113)*

Edward O. Wilson *(p. 101)*

Key People Quiz

Review of Key People – Matching Quiz

1. _____ Believed that in each of the four stages of cognitive development (from birth through adolescence), children's activities are governed by their perceptions of the world around them.
2. _____ Criticized Kohlberg's research for its sole reliance on male subjects, claiming there was evidence of male–female differences with regard to morality.
3. _____ Elaborated on Piaget's work, describing how morality develops.
4. _____ Coined the term "looking-glass self."
5. _____ The founder of psychoanalytic theory.
6. _____ Described how the self develops, and divided the self into the "I" and the "me."
7. _____ Pioneered sociobiology, arguing that genetic inheritance underlies many forms of social behaviour.
8. _____ Divided occupational socialization into four phases.

a. Charles Horton Cooley
b. Sigmund Freud
c. Carol Gilligan
d. Lawrence Kohlberg
e. George Herbert Mead
f. Wilbert Moore
g. Jean Piaget
h. Edward O. Wilson

Learning Objectives

After reading Chapter 4, the student should be able to:

1. define socialization and explain why this process is essential for the individual and society (p. 99).
2. distinguish between sociological and sociobiological perspectives on the development of human behaviour (pp. 100–101).
3. explain why cases of isolated children are important to our understanding of the socialization process (pp. 101–103).

4. understand how child maltreatment is implicated in the process of socialization (pp. 102–104).

5. be able to list the major agents of socialization (pp. 104–08)

6. describe how the family and the school system affect children's development (pp. 104–06).

7. describe the socializing roles of peer groups and the mass media (pp. 106–08).

8. understand what is meant by the notions of "self-concept" and "self-identity" (p. 108).

9. define Charles Horton Cooley's notion of the "looking-glass self" and explain how the looking-glass self develops (pp. 108–109).

10. explain the importance of "role-taking" and "significant others" to George Herbert Mead's theory of human development (pp. 109–111).

11. be able to list and describe the three stages in the development of the self according to George Herbert Mead (pp. 110–111).

12. identify some of the strengths and weaknesses of Cooley and Mead's approaches to socialization (p. 111).

13. note how recent symbolic interactionist perspectives describe childhood as a socially constructed category (p. 111).

14. be able to list and describe the three components of personality central to Sigmund Freud's psychoanalytical perspective (pp. 112–113).

15. outline the stages of cognitive development as set forth by Jean Piaget (p. 113).

16. describe and distinguish between Lawrence Kohlberg's three stages of moral development (pp. 113–114).

17. compare and contrast Lawrence Kohlberg and Carol Gilligan's theories of moral development (pp. 113–114).

18. explain what is meant by gender socialization (pp. 114–15).

19. outline the stages of the life course and note identifying characteristics of each stage (pp. 115–18).

20. describe voluntary and involuntary resocialization processes (pp. 118–20).

Unit Mastery Quizzes

Unit Mastery – Multiple Choice

1. In which of Mead's stages of development does a child learn to use language and other symbols, taking on roles of others including a "doctor" or "superhero"?
   a. preparatory
   b. play
   c. game
   d. moral

2. The _____ would claim "I want that candy bar, no matter what!" according to Freud's theory of personality.
   a. id
   b. ego
   c. superego
   d. conscience

3. Which of the following is a major agent of socialization?
   a. the family
   b. mass media
   c. peer groups
   d. all of the above are agents of socialization.

4. The symbolic interactionist perspective:
   a. emphasizes that socialization is a collective process in which children are active and creative agents.
   b. contends that childhood is a socially constructed category.
   c. notes that children are capable of actively constructing their own shared meanings as they acquire language skills and accumulate interactive experiences.
   d. would note all of the above in relation to the socialization of children.

5. Peer groups function as agents of socialization primarily by:
   a. contributing to our sense of "belonging" and self-worth.
   b. transmitting cultural and social values to us.
   c. providing an array of viewpoints on current issues.
   d. introducing us to a wide variety of people.

6. Which of the following statements about socialization is FALSE?
   a. Socialization is essential for human development.
   b. Socialization is a lifelong process.
   c. The content of socialization is basically the same from one society to another.
   d. The socialization process is more effective when people conform to the norms of society.

7. Our perception of what kind of person we are is known as our:
   a. ego.
   b. id.
   c. self-concept.
   d. self-identity.

8. A sociobiologist is most likely to argue that:
   a. socialization determines what kind of person we become.
   b. peer groups are the most important agent of socialization.
   c. behaviour is largely the result of genetics.
   d. social isolation has a detrimental effect on nonhuman primates.

9. All of the following form the basis of Kohlberg's stages of moral development EXCEPT the:
   a. preconventional level.
   b. formal level.
   c. conventional level.
   d. postconventional level.

10. The cases of "Anna" and "Genie" illustrate that:
    a. successful socialization results in the absence of human contact.
    b. the effects of social isolation on humans cannot be determined with any accuracy.
    c. the behaviour of humans is totally dissimilar to that of nonhuman primates.
    d. socialization is unsuccessful in the absence of early social interaction.

11. The looking-glass self is:
    a. who we actually are.
    b. what people actually think of us.
    c. based on our perception of how other people think of us.
    d. our perception about what kind of person we are.

12. _____ emphasized the role of significant others in the development of the self.
    a. Charles Horton Cooley
    b. George Herbert Mead
    c. Sigmund Freud
    d. Jean Piaget

13. Military boot camps, prisons, concentration camps, and some mental hospitals are examples of:
    a. resocialization agents.
    b. total institutions.
    c. socialization agents.
    d. retribution agents.

14. Which of the following statements best summarizes how child maltreatment is implicated in the process of socialization?
    a. Child abuse rises in direct proportion to the number of one-parent families in society.
    b. A child's self-concept develops in the absence of interactions with others.
    c. If individuals do not learn appropriate models of parenting from their own families, then it can be difficult to learn them elsewhere.
    d. Parents who were abused as children never abuse their own children.

15. Anticipatory socialization practices are most closely associated with which stage in the life course?
    a. infancy and childhood
    b. adolescence
    c. middle adulthood
    d. older adulthood

16. Which of the following is NOT a major criticism of Cooley and Mead's theories of human development?
    a. Cooley's idea of the looking-glass self makes us aware that our perception of how we think others see us is not always correct.
    b. The theories are excessively conservative because they assume that what is good for dominant group members is good for everyone.
    c. There is no allowance for conflict between the "I" and the "me," which are both essential to the formation of the social self.
    d. People may be viewed as "deficient" or "poorly adjusted" if they do not accept uncritically the core values, norms, and behaviours of mainstream society.

17. In which of Piaget's developmental stages can children draw conclusions about the likely physical consequences of an action without always having to try it out?
    a. sensorimotor
    b. preoperational
    c. concrete operational
    d. formal operational

18. Responding differently to male and female infants by playing more roughly with boys and talking more lovingly to girls illustrates:
    a. social devaluation.
    b. anticipatory socialization.
    c. gender socialization.
    d. total institution.

19. According to functionalists, schools are responsible for:
    a. teaching students to be productive members of society.
    b. transmitting culture.
    c. social control and personal development.
    d. all of the above.

20. Carol Gilligan's research:
    a. highlights the need to be aware of the possibility that some theories about human development may not be equally applicable to males and females.
    b. shows that social isolation and neglect are extremely detrimental to young children.
    c. shows the effects of isolation on nonhuman primates.
    d. stressed the importance of play and games, as children try out different roles and gain an appreciation of them.

Unit Mastery − True or False

1. Sociobiologists focus on how humans design their own culture and transmit it from generation to generation through socialization (p. 101).
   TRUE or FALSE

2. When a person is well adjusted, the ego successfully manages the opposing forces of the id and the superego (p. 113).

   TRUE or FALSE

3. During Mead's play stage, children understand not only their own social position but also the positions of others around them (p. 110).

   TRUE or FALSE

4. Child abuse includes physical abuse, sexual abuse, physical neglect, and emotional mistreatment (p. 102).

   TRUE or FALSE

5. Socialization ends in older adulthood (p. 99).

   TRUE or FALSE

6. Cooley asserted that we base our perception of who we are on how we think other people see us and on whether this seems good or bad to us (p. 108).

   TRUE or FALSE

7. Everyone goes through stages of a life course at the same age (pp. 117–118).

   TRUE or FALSE

8. Involuntary resocialization occurs against a person's wishes and generally takes place within a total institution (pp. 119–120).

   TRUE or FALSE

9. Currently, approximately 70 percent of Canadian preschool children are in daycare, in either private homes or institutional settings (p. 105).

   TRUE or FALSE

10. In the future, the family is likely to remain the institution that most fundamentally shapes and nurtures personal values and self-identity (p. 120).

    TRUE or FALSE

Unit Mastery – Fill In the Blanks

1. The family, the school, peer groups, and the mass media are _____ of _____ (p. 104).

2. The _____ - _____ _____ is based on our perception of how other people think of us (p. 108).

3. During the _____ _____ , up to about age 3, interactions lack meaning, and children largely imitate the people around them (p. 110).

4. _____ is essential for an individual's survival and for human development (p. 99).

5. _____ socialization is one of the most important types of adult socialization (p. 117).

6. In early childhood, _____ _____ are often composed of classmates in daycare, preschool, and elementary school (p. 106).

7. The _____ _____ are composed of large-scale organizations that use print or electronic means to communicate with large numbers of people (p. 106).

8. The new-born baby's personality is all _____ , and from birth, the child finds that urges for self-gratification are not going to be satisfied immediately (p. 112).

9. Mead extended Cooley's insights by linking the idea of self-concept to _____ (the process by which a person mentally assumes the role of another) (p. 109).

10. Our _____ is our perception about what kind of person we are (p. 108).

Unit Mastery – Matching Quiz

Match the concept with the appropriate theorist:

1. _____ Sigmund Freud
2. _____ Charles Cooley
3. _____ Lawrence Kohlberg
4. _____ Jean Piaget
5. _____ George Herbert Mead

a. looking-glass self
b. superego
c. generalized other
d. conventional level
e. formal operational stage

Unit Mastery – Matching Quiz 2

Match Piaget's stage of development with its main characteristics.

1. _____ Children begin to use words as mental symbols and to form mental images. However, they are still limited in their ability to use logic to solve problems.

2. _____ Adolescents have the potential to engage in highly abstract thought and understand places, things, and events they have never seen.

3. _____ Children think in terms of tangible objects and actual events. They can draw conclusions about the likely sequences of an action without always having to try the action out.

4. _____ Children understand the world only through sensory contact and immediate action.

a. Sensorimotor
b. Preoperational
c. Concrete operational
d. Formal operational

Solutions

Key Terms Quiz

Review of Key Terms − Fill In the Blanks

1. Social devaluation
2. Supergo
3. Ego
4. Id
5. Sociobiology
6. Generalized other
7. Peer group
8. Socialization
9. Role-taking
10. Significant others
11. Looking-glass self
12. Agents of socialization
13. Gender socialization
14. Resocialization
15. Self-concept
16. Total institution
17. Anticipatory socialization

Key People Quiz

Review of Key People − Matching Quiz

1. G
2. C
3. D
4. A
5. B
6. E
7. H
8. F

Unit Mastery Quizzes

Unit Mastery − Multiple Choice

1. B
2. A
3. D
4. (D)
5. A
6. (C)
7. D
8. C
9. B
10. D
11. C
12. B
13. B
14. C
15. B
16. A
17. C
18. C
19. D
20. A

Unit Mastery − True or False

1. F, Sociobiologists assert that nature, in the form of our genetic makeup, is a major factor in shaping human behaviour.
2. T
3. F, In the play stage, children learn to use language and other symbols, which enable them to pretend to take the roles of specific people. At this stage, children begin to see themselves in relation to others.
4. T
5. F, Socialization is a life-long process of social interaction.
6. T
7. F, Not everyone goes through passages or stages of a life course at the same age (and life course patterns are strongly influenced by ethnicity and social class as well).
8. T
9. T
10. T

Unit Mastery − Fill In the Blanks

1. agents; socialization
2. looking; glass self
3. preparatory stage
4. Socializaton
5. Workplace
6. peer groups
7. mass media
8. id
9. role-taking
10. self-identity

Unit Mastery − Matching Quiz

1. B
2. A
3. D
4. E
5. C

Unit Mastery − Matching Quiz 2

1. B
2. D
3. C
4. A

Society, Social Structure, and Interaction

Chapter Outline

Chapter Summary

Social structure and interaction are critical components of everyday life. At the microlevel, social interaction—the process by which people act toward or respond to other people—is the foundation of meaningful relationships. At the macrolevel, social structure is the stable pattern of social relationships that exists within a particular group or society. This structure includes social institutions, groups, statuses, roles, and norms. Changes in social structure may dramatically affect individuals and groups, as demonstrated by Durkheim's concepts of mechanical and organic solidarity and Tönnies' *Gemeinschaft* and *Gesellschaft*.

Social interaction within a society is guided by shared meanings of how we behave while our perception of those meanings is influenced by race, ethnicity, gender, and social class. The social construction of reality refers to the process by which our perception of reality is shaped by the subjective meaning we give to an experience. Ethnomethodology is the study of the commonsense knowledge that people use to understand the situations in which they find themselves. Dramaturgical analysis is the study of social interaction that compares everyday life to a theatrical presentation. Presentation of self refers to efforts to present our own self to others in ways that are most favourable to our own interests or image. Feeling rules shape the appropriate emotions for a given role or specific situation. Social interaction is also marked by nonverbal communication, which is the transfer of information between people without the use of speech. As we enter the future, macrolevel and microlevel analyses are essential in the determination of how our social structures should be shaped so that they can respond to pressing needs.

Key Terms

achieved status *(p. 129)*

ascribed status *(p. 129)*

dramaturgical analysis *(p. 143)*

ethnomethodology *(p. 141)*

formal organization *(p. 135)*

Gemeinschaft *(p. 137)*

Gesellschaft *(p. 137)*

impression management *(p. 143)*

master status *(p. 129)*

mechanical solidarity *(p. 137)*

nonverbal communication *(p. 145)*

organic solidarity *(p. 137)*

personal space *(p. 147)*

primary group *(p. 134)*

relative homelessness *(p. 126)*

role *(p. 131)*

role conflict *(p. 131)*

role exit *(p. 133)*

role expectation *(p. 131)*

role performance *(p. 131)*

role strain *(p. 132)*

secondary group *(p. 134)*

self-fulfilling prophecy *(p. 141)*

social construction of reality *(p. 141)*

social group *(p. 134)*

social institution *(p. 136)*

social interaction *(p. 125)*

social marginality *(p. 128)*

social network *(p. 134)*

social structure *(p. 125)*

status *(p. 129)*

status set *(p. 129)*

status symbol *(p. 130)*

stigma *(p. 128)*

Key Terms Quiz

Review of Key Terms – Fill In the Blanks

1. _____ _____ is a group's or society's definition of the way a specific role *ought* to be played.

2. _____ _____ is how a person *actually* plays a role in society.

3. _____ _____ is a material sign that informs others of a person's specific status.

4. _____ _____ occurs when incompatible role demands are placed on a person by two or more statuses held at the same time.

5. _____ _____ occurs when incompatible demands are built into a single status that a person occupies.

6. A _____ _____ is a series of social relationships that link an individual to others.

7. A _____ _____ is a set of organized beliefs and rules that establish how a society will attempt to meets its basic social needs.

8. A _____ _____ is a highly structured group formed for the purpose of completing certain tasks or achieving specific goals.

9. _____ is a large urban society in which social bonds are based on impersonal and specialized relationships, with little long-term commitment to the group or consensus on values.

10. _____ _____ is the transfer of information between persons without the use of speech.

11. _____ _____ is the study of social interaction that compares everyday life to a theatrical presentation.

12. _____ is the study of the commonsense knowledge that people use to understand the situations in which they find themselves.

13. _____ _____ are people's efforts to present themselves to others in ways that are most favourable to their own interests or image.

14. _____ _____ is the social cohesion found in industrial societies, in which people perform very specialized tasks and feel united by their mutual dependence.

15. _____ is a traditional society in which social relationships are based on personal bonds of friendship and kinship and on intergenerational stability.

16. _____ _____ is the stable pattern of social relationships that exist within a particular group or society.

17. _____ _____ is the process by which people act toward or respond to other people and is the foundation for all relationships and groups in society.

18. _____ _____ is a social position conferred at birth or received involuntarily later in life.

19. _____ _____ is a social position a person assumes voluntarily as a result of personal choice, merit, or direct effort.

20. A _____ _____ is the most important status a person occupies; it dominates all of the individual's other statuses.

21. _____ _____ is the social cohesion in preindustrial societies, in which there is minimal division of labour and people feel united by shared values and common social bonds.

22. _____ is a socially defined position in a group or society characterized by certain expectations, rights, and duties.

23. _____ _____ includes all the statuses that a person occupies at a given time.

24. _____ is any physical or social attribute or sign that so devalues a person's social identity that it disqualifies that person from full social acceptance.

25. A _____ _____ consists of two or more people who interact frequently and share a common identity and a feeling of interdependence.

26. _____ _____ is the state of being part insider and part outsider in the social structure.

27. _____ _____ _____ _____ is the process by which our perception of reality is shaped largely by the subjective meaning that we give to an experience.

28. A _____ _____ is a larger, more specialized group in which members engage in more impersonal, goal-oriented relationships for a limited period of time.

29. A _____ _____ is a small, less specialized group in which members engage in face-to-face, emotion-based interactions over an extended period of time.

30. _____ _____ is the immediate area surrounding a person that the person claims is private.

31. A _____ is a set of behavioural expectations associated with a given status.

32. _____ _____ occurs when people disengage from social roles that have been central to their self-identity.

33. A _____ _____ is a false belief or prediction that produces behaviour that makes the originally false belief come true.

34. _____ homelessness involves being housed in a dwelling that fails to meet basic living standards.

Key People

Daniel and Cheryl Albas *(p. 143)*

Emile Durkheim *(p. 137)*

Harold Garfinkel *(p. 141)*

Erving Goffman *(p. 143)*

Edward Hall *(p. 147)*

Arlie Hochschild *(p. 144)*

Ferdinand Tönnies *(p. 137)*

Jacqueline Wiseman *(p. 141)*

Key People Quiz

Review of Key People – Matching Quiz

1. _____ Suggested that people acquire feeling rules that shape our emotions in a given situation.

2. _____ Analyzed how students present themselves and manage impressions when exam grades are returned.

3. _____ Was critical of mainstream sociology for not recognizing the ways in which people create their own reality.

4. _____ Used the terms *Gemeinschaft* and *Gesellschaft* to characterize the degree of social solidarity and social control found in societies.

5. _____ Found that homeless people living on skid row evaluated their situation more positively than the social workers who dealt with them.

6. _____ Suggested that day-to-day interactions have much in common with being on stage or in a dramatic production.

7. _____ Analyzed the physical distance between people speaking to one another and found that the amount of personal space people prefer varies from one culture to another.

8. _____ Asserted that preindustrialized societies were held together by strong tradition and by shared moral beliefs and values.

a. Daniel and Cheryl Albas
b. Emile Durkheim
c. Harold Garfinkel
d. Erving Goffman
e. Edward Hall
f. Arlie Hochschild
g. Ferdinand Tönnies
h. Jacqueline Wiseman

Learning Objectives

After reading Chapter 5, the student should be able to:

1. state the definition of social interaction and social structure and explain why these concepts are important for individuals and society (pp. 125–26).

2. explain what is meant by "social marginality" and "stigma" and describe the relationship between these terms (pp. 128–29).

3. state the definition of status and distinguish between ascribed and achieved statuses (p. 129).

4. explain what is meant by "master status" and provide an example of one (pp. 129–30).

5. define "role" and note the difference between role expectation and role performance (p. 131).

6. understand the difference between role conflict and role strain, and be able to provide an example of each (pp. 131–32).

7. describe the process of role exiting (p. 133).

8. explain the difference in primary and secondary groups (p. 134).

9. define formal organization and explain why many contemporary organizations are known as "people-processing" organizations (p. 135).

10. state the definition for social institution and name the major institutions found in contemporary society (p. 136).

11. evaluate functionalist and conflict perspectives on the nature and purpose of social institutions (p. 136).

12. compare Emile Durkheim's typology of mechanical and organic solidarity with Ferdinand Tönnies' *Gemeinschaft* and *Gesellschaft* (p. 137).

13. explain what symbolic interactionists mean by the social construction of reality (pp. 140–41).

14. describe ethnomethodology and note its strengths and weaknesses (pp. 141–43).

15. describe Goffman's dramaturgical analysis (p. 143).

16. explain Goffman's notion of "face-saving behaviour" and provide an example that illustrates how face-saving behaviour operates in everyday life (p. 144).

17. explain what is meant by the sociology of emotions and describe sociologist Arlie Hochschild's contribution to this area of study (pp. 144–45).

18. define nonverbal communication and explain why it is important in social interactions (pp. 145–46).

19. state the definition for personal space and describe the "distance zones" identified by Hall (pp. 147–48).

20. describe some of the ways in which our thinking needs to change before we can understand homelessness (p. 148).

Unit Mastery Quizzes

Unit Mastery – Multiple Choice

1. Being wealthy influences many aspects of life, including health, leisure, and education. Being wealthy is:
    a. a status set.
    b. a status role.
    c. a social stigma.
    d. a master status.

2. Which of the following examples best illustrates stigmatization?
   a. A convicted criminal who must wear a prison uniform.
   b. A steel worker who receives a promotion to foreman.
   c. A woman who earns a master's degree in psychology.
   d. A soldier who wears a medal of honour.

3. Durkheim's notion of mechanical solidarity is similar to Tönnies' notion of:
   a. *Gesellschaft.*
   b. *Gemeinschaft.*
   c. social marginality.
   d. secondary groups.

4. All of the following are examples of formal organizations EXCEPT:
   a. colleges.
   b. families.
   c. corporations.
   d. government.

5. Ex-convicts, ex-nuns, divorcees, and retirees have all undergone:
   a. master status.
   b. role strain.
   c. dramaturgical analyses.
   d. role exit.

6. Which perspective claims that social institutions maintain the privileges of the wealthy and powerful while contributing to the powerlessness of others?
   a. functional
   b. conflict
   c. symbolic interactionist
   d. dramaturgical

7. A police officer is likely to view the scene of a crime much differently than a criminal or a victim. Symbolic interactionists describe how people define the same situation in different ways as:
   a. the social construction of reality.
   b. face-saving behaviour.
   c. social structure.
   d. self-fulfilling prophecy.

8. John is a father, husband, college graduate, and convicted criminal. This example describes John's:
   a. status symbols.
   b. ascribed statuses.
   c. achieved statuses.
   d. social structure.

9. _____ is essential for the survival of society and for the well-being of individuals because it provides a web of familial support and social relationships that connect each of us to the larger society.
   a. Social interaction
   b. Social structure
   c. Social status
   d. Social space

10. A student who shows up late for class, speaks out of turn, and stands facing the class instead of sitting in her seat has violated:
    a. a status set.
    b. a social network.
    c. role expectations.
    d. status roles.

11. Susan is torn between going to her mother's for supper, spending time with her nephew, or working late at the office. Susan is experiencing:
    a. role conflict.
    b. role strain.
    c. role ambiguity.
    d. role exit.

12. Close friends and family members form the basis of:
    a. *Gemeinschaft.*
    b. *Gesellschaft.*
    c. primary groups.
    d. secondary groups.

13. All of the following are major social institutions EXCEPT:
    a. the family.
    b. religion.
    c. the government.
    d. all of the above are major social institutions.

14. The study of background expectancies such as knowing when it is your turn to speak is the work of:
    a. functionalists.
    b. ethnomethodologists.
    c. conflict theorists.
    d. anthropologists.

15. Which of Hall's (1966) distance zones ranges from 1.2 to 3.6 metres and marks formal relationships?
    a. intimate distance
    b. personal distance
    c. social distance
    d. public distance

16. Sociologist Arlie Hochschild (1983) used the term _____ to describe how we know which emotions are required, acceptable, and unacceptable in a given situation.
    a.   master status
    b.   role emotions
    c.   feeling rules
    d.   face-saving behaviours

17. Impression management refers to people's efforts to:
    a.   rescue their performance after experiencing loss of face.
    b.   compare everyday life to a theatrical presentation.
    c.   understand the situations in which they find themselves.
    d.   present themselves to others in ways most favourable to their own interests.

18. According to the text, an understanding of homelessness requires:
    a.   an examination of structural factors that contribute to personal problems.
    b.   first-hand experience of being homeless.
    c.   a degree in social work.
    d.   learning a new and different set of attitudes, values, and behaviours.

19. Nonverbal communication includes:
    a.   facial expressions.
    b.   head movements.
    c.   body movements.
    d.   all of the above.

20. After receiving a low grade on an exam, Mark claimed that he was ill on the day of the test and that some of the test questions were unfair. This example demonstrates:
    a.   face-saving behaviour.
    b.   role conflict.
    c.   role strain.
    d.   social marginality.

Unit Mastery – True or False

1.   Social interaction is the foundation for all relationships and groups in society (p. 125).
     TRUE or FALSE

2.   Most homeless people choose to be homeless (pp. 127–28).
     TRUE or FALSE

3.   Social marginality results in stigmatization (pp. 128–29).
     TRUE or FALSE

4.   Ethnicity, age, and gender are examples of achieved statuses (p. 129).
     TRUE or FALSE

5.   We occupy a role; we play a status (p. 131).
     TRUE or FALSE

6. Role distancing occurs when people disengage from social roles that have been central to their identity (p. 132).

   TRUE or FALSE

7. Mechanical solidarity is characterized by less personal, more status-oriented interactions that are focused on specific goals (p. 137).

   TRUE or FALSE

8. Our perceptions and behaviour are influenced by how we initially define situations (p. 141).

   TRUE or FALSE

9. The need for impression management is most intense when role players have widely divergent or devalued statuses (p. 144).

   TRUE or FALSE

10. Public distance ranges from 1.2 metres to 3.6 metres, marking formal relationships such as job interviews and business transactions (p. 148).

    TRUE or FALSE

Unit Mastery − Fill In the Blanks

1. We _____ a status, we _____ a role (p. 131).

2. In addition to providing a map for our encounters with others, _____ _____ may limit our options and place us in arbitrary categories not of our own choosing (p. 128).

3. A _____ _____ is made up of all the statuses that a person occupies at a given time (p. 129).

4. A _____ _____ dominates all of the individual's other statuses and is the overriding ingredient in determining a person's general social position (p. 129).

5. Driving a Rolls Royce is a _____ _____ that informs others of the driver's wealth (p. 130).

6. _____ _____ occurs when the expectations associated with a role are unclear (p. 131).

7. A _____ _____ is a small, less specialized group in which members engage in face-to-face, emotion-based interactions over an extended period of time (p. 134).

8. Many of us spend most of our time in _____ _____ , such as universities, corporations, or the government (p. 135).

9. _____ of _____ refers to how the various tasks of a society are divided up and performed (p. 137).

10. _____ _____ (or presentation of self) refers to people's efforts to present themselves

to others in ways that are most favourable to their own interests or images (p. 143).

Unit Mastery − Matching Quiz

Match the concept with its originator:

1. _____ Harold Garfinkel
2. _____ Erving Goffman
3. _____ Emile Durkheim
4. _____ Ferdinand Tönnies
5. _____ Arlie Hoshschild

a. dramaturgical analysis
b. ethnomethodology
c. mechanic and organic solidarity
d. *Gemeinschaft* and *Gesellschaft*
e. feeling rules

Solutions

Key Terms Quiz

Review of Key Terms – Fill In the Blanks

1. Role expectation
2. Role performance
3. Status symbol
4. Role conflict
5. Role strain
6. social network
7. social institution
8. formal organization
9. Gesellschaft
10. Nonverbal communication
11. Dramaturgical analysis
12. Ethnomethodology
13. Impression management
14. Organic solidarity
15. Gemeinschaft
16. Social structure
17. Social interaction
18. Ascribed status
19. Achieved status
20. master status
21. Mechanical solidarity
22. Status
23. Status set
24. Stigma
25. social group
26. Social marginality
27. Social construction of reality
28. secondary group
29. primary group
30. Personal space
31. role
32. Role exit
33. self-fulfilling prophecy
34. Relative

Key People Quiz

Review of Key People – Matching Quiz

1. F
2. A
3. C
4. G
5. H
6. D
7. E
8. B

Unit Mastery Quizzes

Unit Mastery – Multiple Choice

1. D
2. A
3. B
4. B
5. D
6. B
7. A
8. C
9. B
10. C
11. A
12. C
13. D
14. B
15. C
16. C
17. D
18. A
19. D
20. A

Unit Mastery – True or False

1. T
2. F, Homelessness is the result of a number of social factors including poverty, changes in the housing market, and growing rates of unemployment.
3. T
4. F, These are ascribed statuses over which the individual has little or no control.
5. F, We occupy a status; we play a role.
6. F, Role distancing occurs when people consciously foster the impression of a lack of commitment or attachment to a particular role and merely go through the motions of role performance.
7. F, Mechanical solidarity is characterized by minimal division of labour and people feel united by shared values and common social bonds.
8. T
9. T
10. F, Public distance is over 3.6 metres and makes interpersonal communication nearly impossible. Social distance is 1.2 metres to 3.6 metres, marking formal relationships such as job interviews.

Unit Mastery – Fill In the Blanks

1. occupy; play
2. social structure
3. status set
4. master status
5. status symbol
6. Role ambiguity
7. primary group
8. formal organizations
9. Division; labour
10. Impression management

Unit Mastery – Matching Quiz

1. B	2. A
3. C	4. D
	5. E

Groups and Organizations

Chapter Outline

Chapter Summary

Groups are a key element of our social structure and much of our social interaction takes place within them. A social group is a collection of two or more people who interact frequently, share a sense of belonging, and have a feeling of interdependence. Social groups may be either primary groups—small, personal groups in which members engage in emotion-based interactions over an extended period—or secondary groups—larger, more specialized groups in which members have less personal and more formal, goal-oriented relationships. All groups set boundaries to indicate who does and who does not belong: an ingroup is a group to which we belong and with which we identify; an outgroup is a group we do not belong to or perhaps feel hostile toward. The size of a group is one of its most important features. The smallest groups are dyads—groups composed of two members—and triads—groups of three. In order to maintain ties with a group, many members are willing to conform to norms established and reinforced by group members.

A bureaucracy is a formal organization characterized by hierarchical authority, division of labour, explicit procedures, and impersonality in personnel concerns. The iron law of oligarchy refers to the tendency of organizations to become a bureaucracy ruled by the few. In recent times, technology has increased the prevalence of a service economy and has rendered it likely that networks will be the dominant organization of the future.

Key Terms

aggregate *(p. 155)*

bureaucracy *(p. 167)*

bureaucratic personality *(p. 174)*

category *(p. 155)*

conformity *(p. 161)*

dyad *(p. 160)*

goal displacement *(p. 173)*

groupthink *(p. 165)*

informal structure *(p. 170)*

ingroup *(p. 157)*

iron law of oligarchy *(p. 176)*

outgroup *(p. 157)*

rationality *(p. 168)*

reference group *(p. 158)*

small group *(p. 160)*

triad *(p. 161)*

Key Terms Quiz

Review of Key Terms – Fill In the Blanks

1. _____ is the term used for a number of people who may never have met one another but share a similar characteristic (such as education level).

2. _____ is the term used for a group to which a person does not belong and toward which the person may feel a sense of competitiveness or hostility.

3. _____ is the term used for a group to which a person belongs and with which the person feels a sense of identity.

4. _____ is the term used for a collection of people who happen to be in the same place at the same time but share little else in common.

5. _____ _____ is a collectivity small enough for all members to be acquainted with one another and to interact simultaneously.

6. _____ is the process of maintaining or changing behaviour to comply with the norms established by a society, subculture, or other group.

7. _____ _____ describes workers who are more concerned with following correct procedures than they are with getting the job done correctly.

8. _____ is an organizational model characterized by a hierarchy of authority, a clear division of labour, explicit rules and procedures, and impersonality in personal matters.

9. _____ _____ _____ _____ is the tendency to become a bureaucracy ruled by the few.

10. _____ _____ is a group that strongly influences a person's behaviour and social attitudes, regardless of whether that individual is an actual member.

11. _____ is the process by which members of a cohesive group arrive at a decision that many individual members privately believe is unwise.

12. _____ is a group composed of only two members.

13. _____ is the process by which traditional methods of social organization, characterized by informality and spontaneity, gradually are replaced by efficiently administered formal rules and procedures.

14. _____ _____ occurs when rules become an end in themselves rather than a means to an end, and organizational survival becomes more important than achievement of goals.

15. _____ is a group composed of exactly three members.

16. An _____ _____ is composed of those aspects of participants' day-to-day activities and interactions that ignore, bypass, or do not correspond with the official rules and procedures of the bureaucracy.

Key People

Solomon Asch *(p. 162)*

Manuel Castells *(p. 177)*

Charles H. Cooley *(p. 157)*

Irving Janis *(p. 165)*

Robert Michels *(p. 176)*

Stanley Milgram *(p. 162)*

George Ritzer *(p. 176)*

Georg Simmel *(p. 160)*

William Graham Sumner *(p. 157)*

Key People Quiz

Review of Key People − Matching Quiz

1. _____ Examined group decision making among political experts and found that major blunders in U.S. history may be attributed to groupthink.

2. _____ Studied group pressure to conform using estimations of line length.

3. _____ Used the term "primary group" to describe small, less specialized groups in which members engage in face-to-face emotion-based interactions.

4. _____ Used the notion of "iron law of oligarchy" to explain why a small number of leaders at the top make all the important organizational decisions.

5. _____ Coined the term "ingroup" and "outgroup."

6. _____ Studied obedience to authority through willingness to administer electric shocks.

7. _____ Suggested that small groups (e.g., dyads) have distinctive interaction patterns that do not exist in larger groups.

8. _____ Looked at what he called the McDonaldization of society based on efficiency, calculability, predictability, control, and the accompanying irrationalities of rationality.

9. _____ Argues that the old order, based on individual units is being replaced by networks, and we can expect to see more network enterprises in the future.

a. Solomon Asch
b. Charles H. Cooley
c. Irving Janis
d. Robert Michels
e. Stanley Milgram
f. Georg Simmel
g. William Graham Sumner
h. Manuel Castells
i. George Ritzer

Learning Objectives

After reading Chapter 6, the student should be able to:

1. distinguish between aggregates, categories, and groups from a sociological perspective (pp. 154–55).

2. distinguish between primary and secondary groups and explain how people's relationships differ in each (p. 157).

3. distinguish between ingroups and outgroups (p. 157).

4. define reference group and explain its importance (p. 158).

5. define network and note the importance of networks in finding employment (pp. 158–59).

6. describe dyads and triads and explain how interaction patterns change as the size of a group increases (pp. 160–61).

7. describe the findings from Solomon Asch's experiment and explain how these results contribute to our understanding of group conformity (p. 162).

8. briefly describe the procedures and findings of Stanley Milgram's research, noting how the results contribute to our understanding of conformity (pp. 162–65).

9. explain how group conformity is implicated in sexual harassment (p. 165).

10. understand what is meant by groupthink and discuss reasons why it can be dangerous for organizations (pp. 165–67).

11. be able to define bureaucracy and summarize Max Weber's perspective on rationality (pp. 167–68).

12. be able to list and describe the formal characteristics of bureaucracy (pp. 169–70).

13. describe the informal structure in bureaucracies and list its positive and negative aspects (pp. 170–72).

14. discuss how inefficiency and rigidity lead to problems for bureaucratic administrators and workers (pp. 172–74).

15. highlight the major shortcomings of bureaucracies in resisting change (pp. 174–75).

16. note how bureaucratic inefficiency contributes to terrorist attacks (box, pp. 174–75).

17. describe the iron law of oligarchy and explain why bureaucratic hierarchies and oligarchies go hand in hand (p. 176).

18. outline the elements that make up Ritzer's McDonaldization (p. 176).

19. explain what is meant by the term "disintermediation" and note the implications for various industries (box, pp. 182–83).

20. describe network organizations of the future. Be sure to describe critical factors in the development of widely dispersed network organizations (pp. 177–83).

Unit Mastery Quizzes

Unit Mastery – Multiple Choice

1. Suppose you play for the Edmonton Oilers hockey team. In this case, the Calgary Flames team would be considered your:
   a. primary group.
   b. ingroup.
   c. outgroup.
   d. aggregate.

2. A large, impersonal, goal-oriented group is a(n):
   a. dyad.
   b. ingroup.
   c. primary group.
   d. secondary group.

3. A(n) _____ is a web of social relationships that links one person with other people and, through them, with additional other people those people know.
   a. outgroup
   b. reference group
   c. network
   d. secondary group

4. The group decision-making process that results in unwise judgments is called:
   a. coercion.
   b. the Hawthorne effect.
   c. groupthink.
   d. bureaucracy.

5. John Pryor's (1992) experiments on the social dynamics of harassment showed that:
   a. When given the opportunity to do so, only 10 percent of the participants sexually harassed a victim.
   b. Males were more likely to be victims of sexual harassment than females.
   c. Women and men were equally likely to be perpetrators of sexual harassment.
   d. Men who believed that sexual harassment was condoned harassed a female victim in 90 percent of the experiments.

6. A reference group is:
   a. a group that strongly influences a person's behaviour and social attitudes, regardless of whether that individual is an actual member.
   b. a group to which a person does not belong and toward which the person may feel a sense of competitiveness or hostility.
   c. a group composed of exactly three members.
   d. a collectivity small enough for all members to be acquainted with one another and to interact simultaneously.

7. Shoppers in a department store and passengers on a bus are examples of a(n):
   a. category.
   b. aggregate.
   c. primary group.
   d. ingroup.

8. Asch's research using line length showed that group pressure is influenced by:
   a. size of the group.
   b. degree of social cohesion.
   c. size of the group AND degree of social cohension.
   d. none of the above.

9. In a bureaucracy, information often spreads faster through the "grapevine" than through official channels. This illustrates:
   a. hierarchy of authority.
   b. inefficiency and rigidity.
   c. informal structures in bureaucracies.
   d. impersonality in bureaucracies.

10. Married couples form the basis of a(n):
    a. category.
    b. dyad.
    c. secondary group.
    d. outgroup.

11. Stanley Milgram conducted a series of experiments to:
    a. understand the circumstances surrounding sexual harassment.
    b. answer questions about people's obedience to authority.
    c. see if participants would contradict their own best judgment if the rest of the group disagreed with them.
    d. examine group discussion and decision making.

12. The process by which traditional methods are replaced by efficiently administered formal rules is:
    a. bureaucracy.
    b. rationality.
    c. utilitarianism.
    d. coercion.

13. Which of the following is NOT one of formal characteristics of bureaucracy?
    a. hierarchy of authority.
    b. specialization in the division of labour.
    c. standard rules and regulations.
    d. employment based on favouritism or family connection.

14. A prime example of rigidity in bureaucracy is:
    a. lifetime employment.
    b. quality circles.
    c. information structure.
    d. goal displacement.

15. Which of the following is a major shortcoming of bureaucracies?
    a. inefficiency and rigidity
    b. resistance to change
    c. perpetuation of ethnic, class, and gender inequalities
    d. all of the above are major shortcomings of bureaucracy

16. The concentration of power in the hands of a few is referred to as:
    a. team performance.
    b. humanized bureaucracy.
    c. the iron law of oligarchy.
    d. quality circles.

17. Ritzer's McDonaldization of bureaucracy model includes all of the following elements EXCEPT:
    a. efficiency
    b. control
    c. hierarchy of authority
    d. calculability

18. Closed-mindedness, rationalization, squelching of dissent, and mindguards are all examples of:
    a. symptoms of groupthink.
    b. prior conditions that lead to groupthink.
    c. defective decision making in the process of groupthink.
    d. consequences of groupthink.

19. In Ritzer's McDonaldization of society, control is best illustrated by the fact that:
    a. fast-food restaurants operate like an assembly line where food is cooked, assembled, and served according to a standardized procedure.
    b. there is an emphasis on speed and quantity rather than quality.
    c. standard menus and scripted encounters with staff make the experience predicable for customers.
    d. fast-food restaurants never allow individual employees much discretion; instead employees must follow detailed procedures.

20. Castells uses the term _____ to refer to a new type of economic organization where companies or parts of companies join together for specific projects that become the focus of the network.
    a. geodesics
    b. network enterprise
    c. rationality
    d. reference groups

Unit Mastery − True or False

1. All groups set boundaries by distinguishing between insiders who are members and outsiders who are not (p. 157).

   TRUE or FALSE

2. As the size of a group increases beyond three people, members tend to specialize in different tasks, and everyday communication patterns change (p. 161).

   TRUE or FALSE

3. Pryor's research showed that sexual harassment is more likely to occur when it is encouraged by others (p. 165).

   TRUE or FALSE

4. An outgroup is a group to which a person belongs and with which that person feels a sense of identity (p. 157).

   TRUE or FALSE

5. Bureaucratic organizations are characterized by disciplined workers so there are very informal levels of authority and little need for explicit rules and procedures (p. 167).

   TRUE or FALSE

6. Prior conditions for groupthink include an isolated, cohesive, homogenous decision-making group, lack of impartial leadership, and high stress (figure, p. 166).

   TRUE or FALSE

7. People in aggregates share a common purpose but generally do not interact with one another (p. 155).

   TRUE or FALSE

8. Charles Perrow has noted that all groups with a division of labour are hierarchically structured (p. 169).

   TRUE or FALSE

9. Bureaucracies hire staff members and professional employees on the basis of favouritism, family connections, and other subjective factors not relevant to organizational efficiency (p. 170).

   TRUE or FALSE

10. Goal displacement occurs when the rules become an end in themselves rather than a means to an end (p. 173).

    TRUE or FALSE

Unit Mastery − Fill In the Blanks

1. Cooley used the term _____ _____ to describe a small, less specialized group in which members engage in face-to-face, emotion-based interactions over an extended period of time (p. 157).

2. People in _____ share a common purpose but generally do not interact with one another (p. 155).

3. William Graham Sumner coined the terms _____ and _____ to describe people's feelings toward members of their own and other groups (p. 157).

4. A _____ is a group that consists of only two members (p. 160).

5. An organization's _____ _____ comprises those aspects of participants' day-to-day activities and interactions that ignore, bypass, or do not correspond with the official rules and procedures of bureaucracy (p. 170).

6. _____ is a detached approach used toward clients so that personal feelings do not interfere with organizational decisions (p. 170).

7. All organizations encounter the _____ _____ of _____ , the tendency to become a bureaucracy ruled by the few (p. 176).

8. Workers who are more concerned with following correct procedures than getting the job done are described by the term _____ _____ (p. 174).

9. Poor decisions are likely to result from _____ , the process in which members of a cohesive group arrive at a decision that many individual members privately believe is unwise (p. 165).

10. A _____ is a web of social relationships that links one person with other people and, through them, with other people those people know (p. 158).

Unit Mastery − Matching Quiz 1

Match the theorist with the concept central to his research:

1. _____ compliance
2. _____ groupthink
3. _____ obedience

   a. Stanley Milgram
   b. Solomon Asch
   c. Irving Janis

Unit Mastery − Matching Quiz 2

Match the concept with the primary characteristic:

1. _____ compliance
2. _____ hierarchy of authority
3. _____ irrationalities of rationality
4. _____ defective decision making

   a. group think
   b. group conformity
   c. bureaucracy
   d. McDonaldization

Solutions

Key Terms Quiz

Review of Key Terms – Fill In the Blanks

1. Category
2. Outgroup
3. Ingroup
4. Aggregate
5. Small group
6. Conformity
7. Bureaucratic personality
8. Bureaucracy
9. Iron law of oligarchy
10. Reference group
11. Groupthink
12. Dyad
13. Rationality
14. Goal displacement
15. Triad
16. informal structure

Key People Quiz

Review of Key People – Matching Quiz

1. C
2. A
3. B
4. D
5. G
6. E
7. F
8. I
9. H

Unit Mastery Quizzes

Unit Mastery – Multiple Choice

1. C
2. D
3. C
4. C
5. D
6. A
7. B
8. C
9. C
10. B
11. B
12. B
13. D
14. D
15. D
16. C
17. C
18. A
19. D
20. B

Unit Mastery – True or False

1. T
2. T
3. T
4. F, An ingroup is a group to which a person belongs and with which a person feels a sense of identity. An outgroup is one to which a person does not belong and may feel a sense of competitiveness toward.
5. F, Bureaucracies are characterized by a hierarchy of authority, a clear division of labour, explicit rules and procedures, and impersonality in personnel matters.
6. T
7. T
8. T
9. F, Bureaucracies hire staff members and professional employees on the basis of specific qualifications.
10. T

Unit Mastery – Fill In the Blanks

1. primary group
2. aggregates
3. ingroup; outgroup
4. dyad
5. informal structure
6. Impersonality
7. iron law; oligarchy
8. bureaucratic personality
9. groupthink
10. network

Unit Mastery – Matching Quiz 1

1. B
2. C
3. A

Unit Mastery – Matching Quiz 2

1. B
2. C
3. D
4. A

Crime and Deviance

Chapter Outline

Chapter Summary

All societies have norms to reinforce and help teach acceptable behaviour. They also have social control practices that encourage conformity and discourage deviance (behaviours and beliefs that violate norms). Crime is a form of deviant behaviour that violates criminal law and is punishable by fines, jail terms, and other sanctions. Functionalists use strain theory, opportunity theory, and social bonding theory to argue that socialization into the value of material success without the corresponding legitimate means to achieve that goal accounts for a large portion of crime. Symbolic interactionists use differential association theory and labelling theory to explain how a person's behaviour is influenced by others. The critical perspective suggests that people with economic and political power define as criminal any behaviour that threatens their own interests. Feminist approaches focus on the intertwining of gender, class, race, ethnicity, and deviance. Postmodern perspectives emphasize the connections between power, knowledge, and social control. While the law classifies crime into summary convictions and indictable offences on the basis of its seriousness, sociologists categorize crimes according to how they are committed and how society views them. Four general categories of crime include: conventional, occupational, organized, and political. Studies show that many more crimes are committed than are reported in official statistics. Gender, age, class, and race are key factors in official crime statistics. The criminal justice system includes the police, courts, and prisons—all agencies that have considerable discretion in dealing with deviance. As we move into the future, we need to find new approaches for dealing with crime and delinquency. We also need to ensure an equal justice system for all, regardless of race, class, sex, or age.

Key Terms

corporate crime *(p. 204)*

crime *(p. 191)*

deviance *(p. 189)*

differential association theory *(p. 195)*

illegitimate opportunity structures *(p. 193)*

juvenile delinquency *(p. 191)*

labelling theory *(p. 196)*

moral crusades *(p. 198)*

moral entrepreneurs *(p. 198)*

occupational or white-collar crime *(p. 204)*

organized crime *(p. 205)*

political crime *(p. 206)*

primary deviance *(p. 197)*

punishment *(p. 218)*

secondary deviance *(p. 197)*

social bond theory *(p. 194)*

social control *(pp. 188 − 89)*

strain theory *(p. 191)*

street crime *(p. 204)*

Key Terms Quiz

Review of Key Terms – Fill In the Blanks

1. _____ is any action designed to deprive a person of things of value because of some offence the person is thought to have committed.

2. _____ _____ is a violation of law by young people under the age of 18.

3. _____ _____ is a business operation that supplies illegal goods and services for profit.

4. _____ _____ are systematic practices developed by social groups to encourage conformity and to discourage deviance.

5. _____ _____ _____ holds that the probability that deviant behaviour increases when a person's ties to society are weakened or broken.

6. _____ is an act that violates criminal law and is punishable with fines, jail terms, and other sanctions.

7. _____ _____ _____ are circumstances that provide an opportunity for people to acquire through illegitimate activities what they cannot get through legitimate channels.

8. _____ _____ suggests that deviants are those people who have been successfully labelled as such by others.

9. _____ _____ is illegal or unethical acts involving the misuse of power by government officials, or illegal or unethical acts perpetrated against the government by outsiders seeking to make a political statement, undermine the government, or overthrow it.

10. _____ is any behaviour, belief, or condition that violates cultural norms in the society or group in which it occurs.

11. _____ _____ is a term for illegal acts committed by corporate employees on behalf of the corporation and with its support.

12. _____ _____ includes all violent crime, certain property crimes, and certain morals crimes.

13. _____ _____ _____ states that individuals have a greater tendency to deviate from societal norms when they frequently associate with persons who favour deviance over conformity.

14. _____ _____ is a term for illegal activities committed by people in the course of their employment or in dealing with their financial affairs.

15. _____ _____ claims that people feel strain when they are exposed to cultural goals that they are unable to obtain because they do not have access to culturally approved means of achieving those goals.

16. _____ _____ occurs when a person who has been labelled a deviant accepts that new identity and continues the deviant behaviour.

17. _____ _____ is the initial act of rule-breaking.

18. _____ _____ are people or groups who take an active role in trying to have particular behaviours defined as deviant.

19. _____ _____ are public and media awareness campaigns that help generate public and political support for their causes.

Key People

Margaret Beare *(p. 191)*

Howard Becker *(p. 196)*

William Chambliss *(p. 197)*

Richard Cloward and Lloyd Ohlin *(p. 193)*

Elizabeth Comack *(p. 200)*

Travis Hirschi *(p. 194)*

Edwin Lemert *(p. 197)*

Peter Letkemann *(p. 195)*

Robert Merton *(p. 191)*

Walter Reckless *(p. 194)*

Richard Quinney *(p. 199)*

Edwin Sutherland *(p. 195)*

Daniel Wolf *(p. 196)*

Key People Quiz

Review of Key People – Matching Quiz 1

1. _____ Examined the relationship between women's earlier victimization in their family and their subsequent involvement in crime.
2. _____ Suggested that for deviance to occur people must have access to illegitimate opportunity structures.
3. _____ Has used strain theory to explain the increased involvement of Canadian Mohawks in the organized smuggling during the early 1990s.
4. _____ Used labelling theory to explain how moral entrepreneurs use their own views of right and wrong to establish rules and label others as deviant.
5. _____ Witnessed labelling theory in the response of law enforcement officials to two groups of high school boys: the Saints and the Roughnecks.
6. _____ Developed a social bond theory of deviance that focuses on the elements of attachment, commitment, involvement, and belief.

a. Margaret Beare
b. Howard Becker
c. William Chambliss
d. Richard Cloward and Lloyd Ohlin
e. Elizabeth Comack
f. Travis Hirschi

Review of Key People − Matching Quiz 2

1. _____ An anthropologist who rode with the Rebels bike gang.

2. _____ According to this sociologist, people with economic and political power define as criminal any behaviour that threatens their own interests.

3. _____ Defined primary and secondary deviance within a labelling theory.

4. _____ Developed a theory of social control that states that certain factors draw people toward deviance while others "insulate" them from such behaviour.

5. _____ Developed differential association theory to explain how people learn deviance through social interaction.

6. _____ Developed strain theory to explain how deviance results from the discrepancy between goals and the means to achieve them.

7. _____ Described how a former Canadian penitentiary resident learned the art of safe-cracking.

a. Edwin Lemert
b. Peter Letkemann
c. Robert Merton
d. Walter Reckless
e. Richard Quinney
f. Edwin Sutherland
g. Daniel Wolf

Learning Objectives

After reading Chapter 7, the student should be able to:

1. define deviance and crime and note the most common forms (pp. 189−91).
2. identify the basic assumptions of strain theory (p. 191).
3. identify the basic assumptions of opportunity theory (p. 193).
4. identify the basic assumptions of control theory (p. 194).
5. note the basic principles of differential association theory (pp. 195−96).
6. describe labelling theory and distinguish between primary and secondary deviance (pp. 196−97).
7. note the role of moral entrepreneurs and moral crusaders (p. 198).
8. outline the key features of conflict perspectives on crime and deviance (pp. 199−200).
9. describe feminist perspective on crime and deviance, and be familiar with the recent research in this area (pp. 200−01).
10. explain how a postmodernist might view deviance and social control (p. 201).
11. note the ways that sociologists classify crime (p. 203).
12. describe the kinds of behaviour included in street crimes (p. 204).

13. differentiate between occupational and corporate crime and explain why people who commit such crimes may not be viewed as "criminals." (pp. 204–05).

14. describe organized crime and political crime and explain how each may weaken social control in society (pp. 205–06).

15. explain how official crime statistics are obtained and why official statistics may not be an accurate reflection of the actual crimes committed (pp. 206–08).

16. explain how victimization surveys contribute to our understanding of crime in society (p. 208).

17. describe the five main correlates of crime (i.e., state each correlate and provide a sentence that describes its relationship to crime) (pp. 209–14).

18. describe the criminal justice system and explain how police and courts have considerable discretion in dealing with offenders (pp. 214–18).

19. list and explain the four functions of punishment (pp. 218–19).

20. describe what is meant by "restorative justice" and note the role of community corrections in a restorative justice approach to crime (pp. 219–20).

Unit Mastery Quizzes

Unit Mastery − Multiple Choice

1. Who focuses on how people develop a self-concept and learn conforming behaviour through the process of socialization?
   a. feminists
   b. conflict theorists
   c. symbolic interactionists
   d. labelling theorists

2. According to conflict perspectives:
   a. people learn deviance through social interaction.
   b. people are drawn to deviance by poverty, unemployment, and lack of educational opportunity.
   c. strong bonds to society prevent people from becoming deviant.
   d. the law is used to protect the positions of those in power.

3. Which theory suggests that people must have access to illegitimate means before they can become criminal or deviant?
   a. conflict
   b. opportunity
   c. labelling
   d. feminist

4. Which of the following theories claims that people get frustrated when they are subjected to cultural goals but do not have the means to achieve these goals?
   a. conflict
   b. social control
   c. strain
   d. labelling

5. Which of the following statements is a valid criticism of the conflict approach to deviance and crime?
   a. Conflict theorists examine the relationship between class, race, and crime.
   b. People with economic and political power define as criminal any behaviour which threatens their own interests.
   c. People of all classes share a consensus about the criminality of certain acts.
   d. The poor commit street crimes in order to survive.

6. The idea that behaviour is not deviant in and of itself, but rather is defined as such by a social audience, forms the basis of which theory?
   a. differential association
   b. labelling
   c. feminism
   d. social control

7. A person who drinks too much or loses his or her rent money at a video lottery terminal would be considered:
   a. conventional.
   b. legitimate.
   c. criminal.
   d. deviant.

8. Feminist scholars note that:
   a. the roots of female criminality lie in a social structure that is characterized by inequalities in class, race, and gender.
   b. some female crimes are attributed to women's lack of job opportunities and to stereotypical expectations about what roles women should have in society.
   c. women are exploited by capitalism and patriarchy.
   d. all of the above.

9. The notion that deviant behaviour is minimal when people have strong bonds to families and other social institutions is central to which theory?
   a. strain
   b. labelling
   c. opportunity
   d. social control

10. Which of the following theories rests on the assumption that deviance is learned through social interaction?
    a. differential association
    b. strain
    c. social control
    d. labelling

11. The law divides crime into _____ and _____ offences.
    a. punishable, nonpunishable
    b. indictable, summary conviction
    c. juvenile, adult
    d. primary, secondary

12. Sexual assault and robbery are forms of:
    a. street crimes.
    b. occupational crimes.
    c. corporate crimes.
    d. organized crimes.

13. Which of the following statements concerning official statistics is FALSE?
    a. Official statistics are generated from Canadian Uniform Crime Reports.
    b. Most public information comes from the Canadian Uniform Crime Reports.
    c. Police statistics always underreport the actual amount of crime.
    d. All crime statistics generated from Canadian Uniform Crime Reports are accurate.

14. An employee who overcharges customers for services in order to pocket the extra money has committed a(n):
    a. corporate crime.
    b. occupational crime.
    c. political crime.
    d. organized crime.

15. Which perspective focuses on the correspondence between culturally approved means and goals?
    a. functionalist
    b. symbolic interactionist
    c. feminist
    d. conflict

16. Why do the police have such a high degree of discretion in determining when charges will be laid?
    a. The police have a broad range of responsibilities.
    b. The police are one of the few public agencies open twenty-four hours a day.
    c. The police have the authority to intervene in situations where something must be done immediately.
    d. All of the above factors contribute to discretion in policing.

17. Using authority in an unethical manner for material gain is at the basis of some forms of:
    a. corporate crime.
    b. occupational crime.
    c. political crime.
    d. organized crime.

18. Which of the following is NOT one of the four functions of punishment?
    a. retribution
    b. rehabilitation
    c. restitution
    d. deterrence

19. Which of the following statements concerning major correlates of crime is TRUE?
    a. Aboriginal people are underrepresented in the criminal justice system.
    b. Arrest rates increase with age.
    c. Females are more likely to be offenders than victims.
    d. The age distribution for crime is remarkably stable.

20. Victimization surveys:
    a. often tell us about crimes that were never reported to the police.
    b. always underreport the actual amount of crime.
    c. clearly illustrate when crimes are on the increase.
    d. indicate that adolescents are most likely to break the law.

Unit Mastery − True or False

1. All societies have norms that govern acceptable behaviour (p. 188).
    TRUE or FALSE

2. As a result of high unemployment and lack of legitimate opportunities, many First Nations members turned to smuggling as a source of income (p. 192).
    TRUE or FALSE

3. Opportunity theory claims that the probability of deviant behaviour increases when a person's ties to society are weakened or broken (p. 194).
    TRUE or FALSE

4. Edwin Sutherland's (1939) differential association theory explains how deviance is learned through social interaction (p. 195).
    TRUE or FALSE

5. Primary deviance occurs when a person accepts the deviant label and continues the deviant behaviour (p. 197).
    TRUE or FALSE

6. According to conflict perspectives, people in positions of power maintain their advantage by using the law to protect their own interests (p. 199).
    TRUE or FALSE

7. Feminist scholars have concluded the roots of female criminality lie in a social structure that is characterized by inequalities of class, race, and gender (p. 200).

   TRUE or FALSE

8. Corporate crime consists of illegal activities committed by people in the course of their employment or in dealing with their financial affairs (p. 204).

   TRUE or FALSE

9. Arrests increase from early adolescence, peak in young adulthood, and steadily decline with age (p. 209).

   TRUE or FALSE

10. Deterrence results from restricting offenders so they cannot commit further crimes (p. 218).

    TRUE or FALSE

Unit Mastery − Fill In the Blanks

1. The _____ _____ _____ includes the police, the courts, and prisons (p. 214).

2. _____ seeks to reduce criminal activity by instilling a fear of punishment (p. 218).

3. Our most important source of crime data are the _____ _____ _____ _____ (p. 206).

4. _____ _____ is a business operation that supplies illegal goods and services for profit (p. 205).

5. _____ _____ refers to illegal or unethical acts involving the misuse of power by government officials, or illegal or unethical acts perpetrated against the government by outsiders (p. 206).

6. According to _____ theory, two complementary processes are involved in the definition of deviance. First some people act in a manner contrary to the expectation of others. Second, others disapprove of and try to control this behaviour (p. 196).

7. According to Travis Hirschi (1969), social bonding consists of four elements: _____ to other people, _____ to conventional lines of behaviour such as schooling, _____ in conventional activities, and _____ in the legitimacy of conventional values (p. 194).

8. Rule violations are dealt with through various mechanisms of _____ _____ , practices developed by social groups to encourage conformity and to discourage deviance (pp. 188−89).

9. Richard Cloward and Lloyd Ohlin (1960) have suggested that for deviance to occur people must have access to _____ _____ _____ (p. 193).

10. People feel strain when they are exposed to cultural _____ that they are unable to obtain because they do not have access to culturally approved _____ (p. 191).

Unit Mastery − Matching Quiz 1

Match the concept with the appropriate theory about crime and deviance:

1. _____ strain theory
2. _____ opportunity theory
3. _____ control theory
4. _____ differential association theory
5. _____ labelling theory
6. _____ knowledge as power

a. social interaction
b. primary and secondary deviance
c. illegitimate opportunities
d. cultural goals and means
e. social bonding
f. Panopticon

Unit Mastery − Matching Quiz 2

Match the theory to the appropriate perspective:

1. _____ functional perspective
2. _____ symbolic interactionist perspective
3. _____ conflict perspective
4. _____ early feminist perspective
5. _____ postmodern perspective

a. labelling theory
b. strain theory
c. conflict approach
d. emancipation theory
e. knowledge as power

Solutions

Key Terms Quiz

Review of Key Terms – Fill In the Blanks

1. Punishment
2. Juvenile delinquency
3. Organized crime
4. Social control
5. Social bond theory
6. Crime
7. Illegitimate opportunity structures
8. Labelling theory
9. Political crime
10. Deviance
11. Corporate crime
12. Street crime
13. Differential association theory
14. Occupational crime
15. Strain theory
16. Secondary deviance
17. Primary deviance
18. Moral entrepreneurs
19. Moral crusades

Key People Quiz

Review of Key People – Matching Quiz 1

1. E
2. D
3. A
4. B
5. C
6. F

Review of Key People – Matching Quiz 2

1. G
2. E
3. A

4. D
5. F
6. C
7. B

Unit Mastery Quizzes

Unit Mastery – Multiple Choice

1. C
2. D
3. B
4. C
5. C
6. B
7. D
8. D
9. D
10. A
11. B
12. A
13. D
14. B
15. A
16. D
17. C
18. C
19. D
20. A

Unit Mastery – True or False

1. T
2. T
3. F, Social bond theory holds that the probability of deviant behaviour increases when a person's ties to society are weakened or broken.
4. T
5. F, Secondary deviance occurs when a person who has been labeled deviant accepts that

new identity and continues the deviant behaviour.
6. T
7. T
8. F, Corporate crime consists of illegal activities acts committed by corporate employees on behalf of the corporation and with its support.
9. T
10. F, Social protection results from restricting offenders so they cannot commit further crimes.

Unit Mastery – Fill In the Blanks

1. criminal justice system
2. Deterrence
3. Canadian Uniform Crime Reports
4. Organized crime
5. Political crime
6. labelling
7. attachment; commitment; involvement; belief
8. social control
9. illegitimate opportunity structures
10. goals; means

Unit Mastery – Matching Quiz 1

1. D
2. C
3. E
4. A
5. B
6. F

Unit Mastery – Matching Quiz 2

1. B
2. A

3. C

4. D

5. E

Social Stratification and Class

Chapter Outline

I. Income and Wealth Differences in Canada

    A. Comparing Income and Wealth

II. Distribution of Income and Wealth

    A. Income Inequality

    B. Wealth Inequality

III. Classical Perspectives on Social Class

    A. Karl Marx: Relationship to Means of Production

    B. Max Weber: Wealth, Prestige, and Power

IV. Sociological Models of the Class Structure in Canada

    A. A Weberian Model of Class Structure

    B. A Marxian Model of Class Structure

    C. A New Class Society?

V. Consequences of Inequality

    A. Physical and Mental Health and Nutrition

    B. Education

    C. Crime and Lack of Safety

VI. Poverty in Canada

    A. Who Are the Poor?

    B. Economic and Structural Sources of Poverty

VII. Sociological Explanations of Social Inequality

    A. Functionalist Perspectives

    B. Conflict Perspectives

    C. Feminist Perspectives

    D. Symbolic Interactionist Perspectives

VIII. Social Class in the Future

Chapter Summary

Placement in Canada's class structure is largely a function of income and wealth. Income consists of economic gain derived from wages and salaries while wealth comprises the net difference between people's assets and debts. Most of the wealthy people in Canada are inheritors in generations removed from their original fortune. There are increasing disparities in the distribution of income and wealth among Canadian families with the wealthiest 20 percent accounting for about 40 percent of the total income pie and the poorest receiving just over 5 percent. There are also regional variations with the lowest incomes in the Atlantic provinces and Nunavut.

Karl Marx and Max Weber identify social class as a key determinant of social inequality and change. According to Marx, capitalistic societies are composed of capitalists, who own the means of production, and workers, who sell their labour to the owners. Weber focuses on the interplay of wealth, prestige, and power. Expanding on Weber's analysis, Dennis Gilbert and Joseph A. Kahl's model is based on education, occupation of the family head, and family income dividing Canadians into the upper, middle, working class, working poor, and underclass. Contemporary Marxist models examine class in relation to people's relationship with others in the production process, rendering most employees as part of the working class. Erik Olin Wright classifies workers as capitalist, managerial, small-business, or working. This century includes a new class society in which transnational corporations, high technology, and disposable workers encounter increasingly polarized lines.

Persons with high income or substantial wealth have greater access to goods and services, better housing, more education, and a wider range of medical services. Conversely, poor people are less healthy, have shorter life expectances, access fewer resources, and are more likely to be labelled as criminals in our society. Absolute poverty exists when people do not have the means to secure the basic necessities of life, and relative poverty exists when people may be able to afford basic necessities but are still unable to maintain an average standard of living. There are both economic and structural sources of poverty.

Functionalist perspectives on social inequality view classes as broad groupings of people who share similar levels of privilege based on the occupational structure. According to the Davis–Moore thesis, positions that are most important to society require the most talent and training and must be highly rewarded. Conflict perspectives assume inequality is created and maintained by the dominant group in order to protect its own economic interests. Feminist scholars focus on the combined effect that gender has on social inequality. The symbolic interactionist perspective can help us gain insight into the effects of wealth and poverty on people's lives. If we do nothing, the gap between rich and poor will widen, and social inequality will continue to increase in the future.

Key Terms

absolute poverty *(p. 250)*

alienation *(p. 235)*

class conflict *(p. 235)*

classism *(p. 245)*

feminization of poverty *(p. 253)*

income *(p. 230)*

job deskilling *(p. 255)*

low-income cutoff *(p. 250)*

meritocracy *(p. 256)*

pink-collar occupations *(p. 241)*

power *(p. 237)*
prestige *(p. 237)*
relative poverty *(p. 250)*

socioeconomic status (SES) *(p. 237)*
wealth *(p. 233)*

Key Terms Quiz

Review of Key Terms − Fill In the Blanks

1. _____ _____ _____ is a combined measure that attempts to classify individuals, families, or households in terms of indicators such as income, occupation, and education to determine class location.

2. _____ _____ are relatively low-paying, nonmanual, semiskilled positions primarily held by women such as daycare workers, checkout clerks, etc.

3. _____ _____ exists when people do not have the means to secure the most basic necessities of life.

4. _____ _____ exists when people may be able to afford basic necessities but still are unable to maintain an average standard of living.

5. _____ _____ is a reduction in the proficiency needed to perform a specific job that leads to a corresponding reduction in the wages for that job.

6. _____ is a hierarchy in which all positions are rewarded based on people's ability and credentials.

7. _____ is the value of all of a person's or family's economic assets, including income, personal property, and income-producing property.

8. _____ is the ability of people or groups to achieve their goals despite opposition from others.

9. _____ is the respect with which a person or status position is regarded by others.

10. _____ _____ _____ refers to the trend in which women are disproportionately represented among individuals living in poverty.

11. _____ is a feeling of powerlessness and estrangement from other people and from oneself.

12. _____ _____ is the struggle between the capitalist class and the working class.

13. _____ is the economic gain derived from wages, salaries, income transfers (governmental aid), and ownership of property.

14. _____ is the belief that persons in the upper or privileged class are superior to those in the lower or working class, particularly in regard to values, behaviour, and lifestyles.

15. _____ _____ is the income level at which a family may be in "strained circumstances" because it spends considerably more on the basic necessities of life (food, shelter, and clothing) than the average family.

Key People

Kingsley Davis and Wilbert Moore *(p. 255)*

Karl Marx *(p. 234)*

Diana Pearce *(p. 253)*

Robert Perrucci and Earl Wysong *(p. 245)*

Max Weber *(p. 236)*

Erik Olin Wright *(p. 243)*

Dennis Gilbert and Joseph A. Kahl *(p. 239)*

Key People Quiz

Review of Key People – Matching Quiz 1

1. _____ Developed a structural functional theory of social stratification.

2. _____ Coined the term "feminization of poverty" and explained why women have a higher risk of being poor.

3. _____ Argued that class position is determined by people's relationship to the means of production.

4. _____ Claims that this century is characterized by a new class society in which transnational corporations, high technology, and disposable workers encounter new and increasingly polarized lines.

a. Kingsley Davis and Wilbert Moore
b. Robert Perrucci and Earl Wysong
c. Karl Marx
d. Diana Pearce

Review of Key People − Matching Quiz 2

1. _____ Developed a model of social classes based on education, occupation of family head, and family income.

2. _____ Outlined criteria for placement into a class structure consisting of the capitalist, managerial, small-business, and working classes.

3. _____ Developed a multidimensional approach to social stratification that focused on the interplay among wealth, prestige, and power.

a. Dennis Gilbert and Joseph A. Kahl
b. Max Weber
c. Erik Olin Wright

Learning Objectives

After reading Chapter 8, the student should be able to:

1. define and distinguish between income and wealth (p. 230).
2. describe income inequality in Canada as measured through income quintiles (pp. 231−33).
3. describe wealth inequality in Canada and explain how analysts define the wealthy (pp. 233−34).
4. describe Karl Marx's perspective on class position and class relationships (pp. 234−36).
5. outline Max Weber's multidimensional approach to social stratification and explain how people are ranked on all three dimensions (pp. 236−38).
6. outline Dennis Gilbert and Joseph A. Kahl's mode of social class based on education, occupation of the family head, and family income (pp. 239−42).
7. briefly describe the key characteristics of the upper, middle, working class, working poor, and the underclass in Canada (pp. 239−242).
8. compare and contrast Karl Marx's and Erik Olin Wright's models of class structure (pp. 242−44).
9. describe the key features of Wright's capitalist, managerial, small-business, and working classes (pp. 244−45).
10. describe Robert Perrucci and Earl Wysong's new class society (pp. 245−46).
11. outline some of the key consequences of inequality for physical and mental health, and nutrition (pp. 246−48).
12. explain how inequalities in wealth and income contribute to differential treatment by the criminal justice system (p. 247).
13. explain how inequalities in wealth and income affect educational opportunities (pp. 248−49).
14. outline the consequences of inequality for safety (pp. 249−50).
15. distinguish between absolute and relative poverty (p. 250).

16. describe the characteristics and lifestyle of those who live in poverty in Canada. Be sure to describe the feminization of poverty and explain why two out of three impoverished adults in Canada are women (pp. 251–55).

17. note some of the major economic and structural sources of poverty (p. 255).

18. outline Davis and Moore's explanation of why social stratification exists in Canadian society (pp. 255–56).

19. note the contributions of the conflict and feminist approach to our understanding of inequality (pp. 256–57).

20. outline the key focus of an interactionist perspective and note what the symbolic interactionists can teach us about class-based inequality (pp. 257–58).

Unit Mastery Quizzes

Unit Mastery − Multiple Choice

1. Which approach to social inequality identifies ownership or non-ownership of the means of production as the distinguishing feature of classes?
   a. interactionist
   b. feminist
   c. functional
   d. conflict

2. Suppose you have adequate food and clothing, but you feel poor because your children have fewer toys than those in the rest of the neighborhood. This demonstrates:
   a. absolute poverty.
   b. relative poverty.
   c. substandard poverty.
   d. relational poverty.

3. According to Perrucci and Wysong, the new working class includes:
   a. the comfort class.
   b. the contingent class
   c. the excluded class.
   d. all of the above.

4. Women have a high risk of being poor because:
   a. they bear the major economic burden of raising children.
   b. many are unable to obtain regular, full-time, year-round employment.
   c. of events such as marital separation, divorce, or widowhood.
   d. all of the above increase women's risk of being poor.

5. For Karl Marx, class position is determined by:
   a. people's relationship to the means of production.
   b. the most important positions being filled by the most qualified individuals.
   c. the value of economic assets.
   d. opportunities for advancement within a stratification system.

6. According to Wright's view of modern capitalism, class structure is determined by:
   a. ownership of means of production
   b. purchase of labour of others (employing others)
   c. control of the labour of others
   d. all of the above

7. Which of the following statements about wealth and health is TRUE?
   a. Children born into poor families have the same risk of dying in their first year as middle-class babies.
   b. The poor have shorter life expectancies than other social classes.
   c. Most poor people receive adequate medical care following illness or injury.
   d. Most high-poverty areas have an adequate supply of doctors and medical facilities.

8. According to functionalists, which of the following statements about the education system is TRUE?
   a. The education system is inflexible.
   b. Inequality in education is increasing.
   c. Class, race, and gender are more important to life chances than student ability.
   d. Educational opportunities and life chances are directly linked.

9. Four classes make up Wright's view of modern capitalism. Which of the following is NOT one of these classes?
   a. the small-business class
   b. the managerial class
   c. the privileged class
   d. the working class

10. All of the following are part of Robert Perrucci and Earl Wysong's new working class EXCEPT:
    a. the superclass.
    b. the comfort class.
    c. the contingent class.
    d. the excluded class.

11. Which of the following statements accurately depicts the income distribution in Canada?
    a. The wealthiest 20 percent of households receive about 40 percent of the total income.
    b. The poorest 20 percent of households receive about 20 percent of the total income.
    c. The top 10 percent of households receive about 40 percent of the total income.
    d. The top 10 percent of households receive about 60 percent of the total income.

12. Max Weber's multidimensional approach to social stratification focused on the interplay among all of the following elements EXCEPT:
    a. wealth.
    b. power.
    c. educational attainment.
    d. prestige.

13. Which of the following statements accurately summarizes the Davis–Moore thesis of social stratification?
    a. Some positions are more important for the survival of society than others.
    b. The most important positions must be filled by the most qualified people.
    c. The positions that are most important require scarce talent or extensive training and thus should be the most highly rewarded.
    d. all of the above are central to the Davis–Moore thesis.

14. All of the following are characteristics of the upper class EXCEPT:
    a. The upper class is the wealthiest and most powerful class in Canada.
    b. Children of the upper class are expected to marry within their own class.
    c. The upper class contains an estimated 40–50 percent of Canada's population.
    d. The upper class is divided into upper-upper and lower-upper categories.

15. Which of the following statements about wealth in Canada is FALSE?
    a. Wealth includes property such as buildings, land, farms, cars, and other assets such as money in bank accounts.
    b. Wealth is computed by subtracting all debt obligations and converting the remaining assets into cash.
    c. The majority of the wealthiest people in Canada are inheritors, with some at least three or four generations removed from the original fortune.
    d. Income is more unevenly distributed among the Canadian population than is wealth.

16. An average family income in Canada is:
    a. close to $40,000.
    b. about $51,000.
    c. just over $58,000.
    d. close to $65,000.

17. The wealthy are usually defined:
    a. in relative terms just like poverty is.
    b. as people who earn more than $80,000 a year.
    c. those whose total assets after debt payments are over $250,000.
    d. those with a net worth of at least $1 million.

18. A recent survey of wealth concluded that there is/are:
    a. fewer millionaires in Canada today than ever before in Canadian history.
    b. most recent wealthy Canadians accumulated their net worth within one generation.
    c. less inequality among Canadians all the time due to lack of wage increases.
    d. gross and persistent inequality in the distribution of wealth in Canada.

19. _____ is a feeling of powerlessness and estrangement from other people and from oneself.
    a. Anomie
    b. Relative poverty
    c. Class conflict
    d. Alienation

20. Poverty and low income lead to heart disease because:
    a. people on low incomes live under conditions of material deprivation that produces a cardiovascular heart burden that accumulates over the life span.
    b. living on low incomes creates excessive stress that damages the cardiovascular system.
    c. the stressful conditions associated with low incomes lead to unhealthy behaviours such as smoking.
    d. all of the above.

Unit Mastery − True or False

1. The terms "wealth" and "income" are interchangeable because they mean basically the same thing (p. 230).
   TRUE or FALSE

2. According to Karl Marx, class relationships involve inequality and exploitation (p. 235).
   TRUE or FALSE

3. According to Max Weber, wealth, power, and prestige are separate continuums (p. 238).
   TRUE or FALSE

4. People may have prestige but not wealth (p. 237).
   TRUE or FALSE

5. In a recent national survey of Canadian adults, 80 percent of respondents rated themselves as part of the working class (p. 240).
   TRUE or FALSE

6. The Davis−Moore thesis assumes that social stratification results in meritocracy (p. 256).
   TRUE or FALSE

7. The working class includes pink-collar occupations (p. 241).
   TRUE or FALSE

8. The top part of Perrucci and Wysong's privileged class is called the comfort class (p. 245).
   TRUE or FALSE

9. Functionalist approaches claim that inequality results from the more powerful exploiting the less powerful (p. 256).
   TRUE or FALSE

10. Symbolic interactionists focus on microlevel concerns and usually do not analyze larger structural factors that contribute to inequality and poverty (p. 257).
    TRUE or FALSE

Unit Mastery − Fill In the Blanks

1. According to Weber, wealth, prestige, and _____ are separate continuums on which people can be ranked from high to low (p. 238).

2. The _____ − _____ thesis assumes that social stratification results in meritocracy (p. 256).

3. Fame, respect, honour, and esteem are the most common forms of _____ (p. 237).

4. _____ theory is based on the assumption that social stratification is created and maintained by one group in order to protect and enhance its own economic interests (p. 256).

5. The _____ - _____ class comes from prominent families which possess great wealth that they have held for several generations (p. 239).

6. _____ is the economic gain derived from wages, salaries, income transfers, and ownership of property (p. 230).

7. _____ is the difference between your assets and your debts (p. 230).

8. _____ _____ describes the reduction in the proficiency needed to perform a specific job that goes along with lower wages (p. 255).

9. Perrucci and Wysong's _____ _____ _____ is divided into the comfort class and the contingent class (p. 245).

10. The most accepted and commonly used definition of poverty is Statistics Canada's before-tax _____ - _____ _____ —the income level at which a family spends more than 70 percent of their income on food, clothing, and shelter (p. 250).

Unit Mastery − Matching Quiz 1

Match the theorist with the appropriate concept:

1. _____ feminization of poverty
2. _____ alienation
3. _____ meritocracy
4. _____ the new working class
5. _____ the small-business class

a. Karl Marx
b. Kingsley Davis and Wilbert Moore
c. Diana Pearce
d. Robert Perrucci and Earl Wysong
e. Erik Olin Wright

Unit Mastery – Matching Quiz 2

Match the social class to its class characteristic:

1. _____ includes 40–50 percent of Canada's population
2. _____ includes people with "new money"
3. _____ includes pink-collar occupations
4. _____ includes high unemployment and reliance on assistance programs
5. _____ live just above or just below the poverty line

   a. upper class
   b. middle class
   c. working class
   d. working poor
   e. underclass

Solutions

Key Terms Quiz

Review of Key Terms – Fill In the Blanks

1. Socioeconomic status (SES)
2. Pink-collar occupations
3. Absolute poverty
4. Relative poverty
5. Job deskilling
6. Meritocracy
7. Wealth
8. Power
9. Prestige
10. Feminization of poverty
11. Alienation
12. Class conflict
13. Income
14. Classism
15. Low-income cutoff

Key People Quiz

Review of Key People – Matching Quiz 1

1. A
2. D
3. C
4. B

Review of Key People – Matching Quiz 2

1. A
2. C
3. B

Unit Mastery Quizzes

Unit Mastery – Multiple Choice

1. D
2. B
3. D
4. D
5. A
6. D
7. B
8. D
9. C
10. A
11. A
12. C
13. D
14. C
15. D
16. C
17. C
18. D
19. D
20. D

Unit Mastery – True or False

1. F, Income is economic gain due to wages and salaries, while wealth is the net difference between assets and debts.
2. T
3. T
4. T
5. F, Eighty percent of respondents rated themselves as part of the middle class while an estimated 40 to 50 percent of Canada's population is actually in this class.
6. T
7. T
8. F, The top part of the privileged class is referred to as the superclass.
9. F, Functionalists suggest that important tasks need to be filled by the most qualified individuals and that important tasks may require specialized skills and training that is compensated for with higher rewards.
10. T

Unit Mastery – Fill In the Blanks

1. power
2. Davis; Moore
3. prestige
4. Conflict
5. upper; upper
6. Income
7. Wealth
8. Job deskilling
9. new working class
10. low; income cutoff

Unit Mastery – Matching Quiz 1

1. C
2. A
3. B
4. D
5. E

Unit Mastery – Matching Quiz 2

1. B
2. A
3. C
4. E
5. D

Global Stratification

Chapter Outline

Chapter Summary

Global stratification refers to the unequal distribution of wealth, power, and prestige on a global basis. This distribution of resources is commonly described as "three worlds": First World (advanced industrialized countries), Second World (communist industrial countries), and Third World (little or no industrialization). In addition, the distribution of resources is described in levels (developed or underdeveloped), and in terms of income (low-income economies, middle-income economies, and high-income economies). The unequal distribution of resources between rich and poor countries is growing due to the consequences of debt and foreign aid. Absolute poverty is now defined as living on less than a dollar a day, while relative poverty exists when people may be able to afford the basic necessities but are still unable to maintain an average standard of living; finally, subjective poverty is measured by comparing actual income against the income earner's expectations and perceptions. Average life expectancy is now more than 70 years in 23 countries, but it is 23 years less in low-income countries. Health refers to physical, mental, and social well-being and not merely the absence of disease or infirmity. Billions of people in developing countries do not have proper sanitation, safe water, adequate shelter, and/or access to modern health services, a fact that makes for high rates of infectious diseases.

The United Nations defines a literate person as someone who can, with understanding, both read and write a short, simple statement on his or her everyday life. The adult literacy rate in low-income countries is about half that of high-income countries and even lower for women. Some theorists claim that global wealth and poverty are linked to the level of industrialization and economic development in a society. According to dependency theorists, rich countries have an interest in maintaining the dependent status of poor countries, as this ensures them a source of raw materials and a captive market for manufactured goods. In contrast, world systems theory suggests that what exists under capitalism is a truly global system held together by economic ties. Finally, according to the new international division of labour theory, commodity production is being split into fragments that can be assigned to whichever part of the world can provide the most profitable combination of capital and labour. As we look to the future, we need to consider that poverty is persistent and even growing in some countries, undermining human development and the possibility for socioeconomic change. On the other hand, modern technology and worldwide economic growth might help reduce poverty and increase people's opportunities.

Key Terms

core nations *(p. 286)*

dependency theory *(p. 285)*

modernization theory *(p. 284)*

new international division of labour theory *(p. 287)*

peripheral nations *(p. 286)*

semiperipheral nations *(p. 287)*

social exclusion *(p. 270)*

world systems theory *(p. 286)*

Key Terms Quiz

Review of Key Terms – Fill In the Blanks

1. _____ _____ are dominant capitalist centres characterized by high levels of industrialization and urbanization.

2. _____ _____ are nations that are dependent on core nations for capital, have little or no industrialization (other than what may be brought in by core nations), and have uneven patterns of urbanization.

3. _____ _____ is the process by which certain individuals and groups are systematically barred from access to positions that would enable them to have an autonomous livelihood in keeping with the social standards and values of a given social context.

4. _____ _____ is a perspective that states that global poverty can at least partially be attributed to the fact that the low-income countries have been exploited by the high-income countries.

5. _____ _____ are nations that are more developed than peripheral nations but less developed than core nations.

6. _____ _____ a perspective that links global inequality to different levels of economic development and suggests that low-income economies can move to middle- and high-income economies by achieving self-sustained economic growth.

7. _____ _____ _____ of _____ _____ is a perspective that states that commodity production is being split into fragments that can be assigned to whichever part of the world can provide the most profitable combination of capital and labour.

8. _____ _____ _____ is a perspective that views the capitalist world economy as a global system divided into a hierarchy of three major types of nations—core, semiperipheral, and peripheral—in which upward or downward mobility is conditioned by the resources and obstacles that characterize the international system.

Key People

Andre Gunder Frank *(p. 285)*   **Immanuel Wallerstein** *(p. 286)*

Walt W. Rostow *(p. 284)*

Key People Quiz

Review of Key People − Matching Quiz

1. _____ A modernization theorist who claimed that one of the largest barriers to development in low-income nations was the traditional cultural values held by people, particularly fatalistic beliefs.

2. _____ Criticized modernization theory and argued that all societies are undeveloped at one time, but underdevelopment was a condition created by the imperial powers that had created dependency through their actions.

3. _____ Believed that a country's mode of incorporation into the capitalist work economy is the key feature in determining how economic development takes place in that nation.

a. Andre Gunder Frank
b. Walt W. Rostow
c. Immanuel Wallerstein

Learning Objectives

After reading Chapter 9, the student should be able to:

1. define global stratification (p. 264).
2. distinguish between high-income and low-income countries (p. 264).
3. distinguish between social and economic inequality (p. 265).
4. be able to complete the quiz "How Much Do You Know About Global Wealth and Poverty?" (pp. 265−66)
5. know what the "three worlds" approach is based on and be able to distinguish between the three worlds and provide examples (p. 270).
6. explain what is meant by underdevelopment and underdeveloped nations (pp. 271−72).
7. describe and distinguish between low-income, middle-income, and high-income economies, and provide examples of each (pp. 273−74).
8. note the major problems with foreign debt (p. 274).
9. outline the relationship between foreign aid and global stratification (pp. 274−76).
10. list and describe the various ways to define poverty (pp. 276−77).
11. list the criteria that make up the Human Development Index and note how Canada fares relative to other countries (pp. 277−78).
12. note the life expectancy in high-income countries and compare this to middle and low-income countries (pp. 278−80).

13. define health and note some of the health problems in developing countries (p. 280).

14. explain how the United Nations Educational, Scientific and Cultural Organization defines a literate person (p. 281).

15. describe the relationship between gender and inequality (pp. 281–82).

16. note the major assumptions of Walt W. Rostow's (1971, 1978) modernization theory (p. 284).

17. note the major assumptions of dependency theory (pp. 285–86).

18. distinguish between core nations, peripheral nations, and semiperipheral nations as described by world systems theory (pp. 286–87).

19. note the major assumptions of the new international division of labour theory (pp. 287–88).

20. be familiar with predictions for global inequality in the future and ways to help low-income countries (pp. 288–93).

Unit Mastery Quizzes

Unit Mastery – Multiple Choice

1. Which of the following is measured by comparing the actual income against the income earner's expectations and perceptions?
   a. absolute poverty
   b. relative poverty
   c. subjective poverty
   d. income disparity

2. The unequal distribution of wealth, power, and prestige on a global basis is known as:
   a. global stratification.
   b. global disparity.
   c. global poverty.
   d. global dependency.

3. Which of the following statements is TRUE?
   a. Because of foreign aid and the globalization of trade, the gap between the incomes of people in the poorest countries and the richest countries has narrowed over the past several decades.
   b. The richest fifth of the world's population receives about 50 percent of the total world income.
   c. Although the percentage of the world's people living in absolute poverty has declined over the past decade, the total number of people living in poverty has increased.
   d. The political role of governments in policing the activities of transnational corporations has expanded as companies' operations have become more globalized.

4. "Second World countries" refer to:
   a. advanced industrial countries such as Britain and France.
   b. communist industrial countries such as Poland and China.
   c. poor countries with little or no industrialization.
   d. none of the above.

5. According to the United Nations Human Development Report on global consumption:
    a. the wealthiest 20 percent of the people account for 62 percent of private consumption.
    b. the wealthiest 20 percent of the people account for 86 percent of private consumption.
    c. the poorest 20 percent of the population account for 10 percent of private consumption.
    d. the poorest 20 percent of the population account for 22 percent of private consumption.

6. GNI refers to:
    a. all the goods and services produced in a country in a given year.
    b. the income earned outside the country by individuals or corporations.
    c. the quality of goods and services that can be purchased in a country.
    d. a and b.

7. According to the World Bank, a GNI per capita of $9,386 U.S. dollars or more in 2005 represents a(n):
    a. low-income economy.
    b. middle-income economy.
    c. upper-middle income economy.
    d. high-income economy.

8. Which of the following statements characterizes low-income economies?
    a. About half the world's population lives in a low-income economy.
    b. They are found primarily in Asia and Africa.
    c. Most people in low-income economies engage in agricultural pursuits.
    d. All of the above characterize low-income economies.

9. Which of the following statements characterizes middle-income economies?
    a. Low rates of inflation characterize lower middle-income economies.
    b. More than half of the people in middle-income economies live in poverty.
    c. There are 93 nations with middle-income economies.
    d. Upper-middle income economies have very low levels of indebtedness and lots of resources for fighting poverty.

10. Which of the followings statements describes the implications of borrowing too much money from other countries (i.e., debt)?
    a. Debt repayment and economic restructuring causes massive unemployment, reduces incomes, and leads to soaring prices.
    b. Governments of poor countries lose whatever power they had to control their own economic destinies because they must follow the dictates of the lenders.
    c. Debt repayment takes money that could otherwise be used to provide social services and health care.
    d. All of the above demonstrate the implications of borrowing too much money.

11. Which of the following statements illustrates the problems associated with foreign aid?
    a. A global oversupply of a food such as grain may actually be contributing to famine by destroying the agricultural base of developing countries, making them vulnerable to future food shortages.
    b. Foreign aid can be tied to specific projects or objectives that may meet the interests of the donor country more than the interests of the recipients (e.g., political objectives).
    c. There is not enough aid to help low-income countries solve health, nutrition, and employment problems.
    d. All of the above are problems associated with foreign aid.

12. Which of the following statements about life expectancy is TRUE?
    a. Average life expectancy has increased by about a third in the past three decades.
    b. Average life expectancy has increased by about a quarter in the past three decades.
    c. Average life expectancy has decreased by about a third in the past three decades.
    d. Average life expectancy has stayed the same over the past three decades.

13. Which of the following statements about life expectancy is FALSE?
    a. The average life expectancy at birth of people in middle-income countries remains about 12 years less than that of people in high-income countries.
    b. The life expectancy in of people in low-income nations is as much as 23 years less than that of people in high-income nations.
    c. One major cause of shorter life expectancy in low-income nations is the high rate of infant mortality.
    d. The average life expectancy is now more than 80 years in 23 countries.

14. Which of the following statements on health is FALSE?
    a. Because of their poverty, many people in low-income nations are far from having physical, mental, and social well-being.
    b. According to the World Health Organization, infectious diseases are under control in most nations.
    c. Tobacco smoking has decreased in high-income countries.
    d. Middle-income countries are experiencing a rapid growth in degenerative diseases such as cancer and coronary heart disease.

15. The United Nations Educational, Scientific and Cultural Organization defines a literate person as:
    a. someone who can, with understanding, read a short, simple statement.
    b. someone who can, with understanding, write a short statement about his or her everyday life.
    c. someone who can, with understanding, write his or her own name.
    d. a and b.

16. Which theory claims that a major barrier to development in low-income nations is the traditional values and fatalistic beliefs held by people?
    a. modernization theory
    b. dependency theory
    c. world systems theory
    d. new international division of labour theory

17. Which theory states that global poverty can at least partially be attributed to the fact that low-income countries have been exploited by the high-income countries?
    a. modernization theory
    b. dependency theory
    c. world systems theory
    d. new international division of labour theory

18. According to this theory, commodity production is being split into fragments that can be assigned to whichever part of the world can provide the most profitable combination of capital and labour.
    a. modernization theory
    b. dependency theory
    c. world systems theory
    d. new international division of labour theory

19. According to this theory, the capitalist economy is a global system divided into a hierarchy of three major types of nations: core, semiperipheral, and peripheral, in which upward or downward mobility is conditioned by the resources and obstacles that characterize the international system.
    a. modernization theory
    b. dependency theory
    c. world systems theory
    d. new international division of labour theory

20. Nations that have little or no industrialization and uneven patterns of urbanization are:
    a. core nations
    b. peripheral nations
    c. labour nations
    d. dependent nations

Unit Mastery – True or False

1. Because of foreign aid and the globalization of trade, the gap between the incomes of people in the poorest countries and the richest countries has narrowed over the past several decades (pp. 264–65).
   TRUE or FALSE

2. The political role of governments in policing the activities of transnational corporations has expanded as operations have become more global (pp. 265–66).
   TRUE or FALSE

3. The richest fifth of the world's population receives about 75 percent of the total world income (pp. 265–66).
   TRUE or FALSE

4. The majority of people with incomes below the poverty line live in rural areas (pp. 265–66).
   TRUE or FALSE

5. About half of the world's population lives in low-income economies (p. 272).
   TRUE or FALSE

6. Compared with lower middle-income economies, nations having upper middle-income economies typically have a somewhat higher standard of living and export diverse goods and services ranging from manufactured goods to raw materials and fuels (p. 273).

   TRUE or FALSE

7. Nations with high-income economies dominate the world economy (p. 273).

   TRUE or FALSE

8. Relative poverty exists when people do not have the means to secure the most basic necessities of life (pp. 276–77).

   TRUE or FALSE

9. Rostow's modernization theory includes four stages of economic development (p. 284).

   TRUE or FALSE

10. Dependency theory makes a positive contribution to our understanding of global poverty by pointing out that "underdevelopment" is not necessarily the cause of inequality (p. 286).

    TRUE or FALSE

Unit Mastery – Fill In the Blanks

1. _____ countries are countries characterized by highly industrialized economies; technologically advanced industrial, administrative, and service occupations; and relatively high levels of national and per capita income (p. 264).

2. _____ countries are countries that are undergoing the transformation from an agrarian to an industrial economy and have lower levels of income (p. 264).

3. _____ World countries include advanced industrial countries such as Britain, France, Germany, Japan, and Canada (p. 270).

4. _____ World countries include communist-industrial countries such as Poland and China (p. 270).

5. The term _____ _____ _____ refers to all the goods and services produced in a country in a given year, plus the income earned outside the country by individuals or corporations (p. 271).

6. Many poor women worldwide do not have access to commercial credit and have been trained only in traditionally female skills that produce low wages. These factors contribute to the global _____ _____ _____ , whereby women around the world tend to be more impoverished than men (p. 273).

7. Nations with high-income _____ continue to dominate the world economy (p. 273).

8. _____ _____ is defined as living on less than a dollar a day (p. 276).

9. _____ _____ exists when people may be able to afford basic necessities but are still unable to maintain an average standard of living (pp. 276–77).

10. The second stage of modernization theory is called the _____ stage, a period of economic growth accompanied by a growth in individualism, competition, and achievement (p. 284).

11. _____ is defined as a state of complete physical, mental, and social well-being and not merely the absence of disease or infirmity (p. 280).

12. _____ _____ are dominant capitalist centres characterized by high levels of industrialization and urbanization (p. 286).

Unit Mastery – Matching Quiz 1

Match the type of economy to the appropriate defining feature:

1. _____ are going through a transition toward a market economy
2. _____ are found primarily in countries in Asia and Africa, where half the world's population resides
3. _____ dominate the world economy

a. low-income economies
b. middle-income economies
c. high-income economies

Unit Mastery – Matching Quiz 2

Match the key concept with the appropriate theory:

1. _____ modernization theory
2. _____ dependency theory
3. _____ world systems theory
4. _____ new international labour theory

a. free trade
b. core nations
c. newly industrializing countries
d. traditional stage

Solutions

Key Terms Quiz

Review of Key Terms – Fill In the Blanks

1. Core nations
2. Peripheral nations
3. Social exclusion
4. Dependency theory
5. Semiperipheral nations
6. Modernization theory
7. New international division; labour theory
8. World systems theory

Key People Quiz

Review of Key People – Matching Quiz

1. B
2. A
3. C

Unit Mastery Quizzes

Unit Mastery – Multiple Choice

1. C
2. A
3. C
4. B
5. B
6. D
7. D
8. D
9. C
10. D
11. D
12. A
13. D
14. B
15. D
16. A
17. B
18. D
19. C
20. B

Unit Mastery – True or False

1. F, Between 1960 and 2000, the gap in global income differences between rich and poor countries continued to widen.
2. F, As companies have globalized their operations, governmental restrictions have become less effective in controlling their activities.
3. T
4. T
5. T
6. T
7. T
8. F, Absolute poverty exists when people can't meet basic needs.
9. T
10. T

Unit Mastery – Fill In the Blanks

1. High-income
2. Low-income
3. First
4. Second
5. gross national income
6. feminization of poverty
7. economies
8. Absolute poverty
9. Relative poverty
10. take-off
11. Health
12. Core nations

Unit Mastery – Matching Quiz 1

1. B
2. A
3. C

Unit Mastery – Matching Quiz 2

1. D
2. C
3. B
4. A

Race and Ethnicity

Chapter Outline

Chapter Summary

Issues of race and ethnicity permeate all levels of interaction in Canada. A race is a category of people who have been singled out as inferior or superior, often on the basis of physical characteristics such as skin colour, hair texture, and eye shape. By contrast, an ethnic group is a collection of people who, as a result of their shared cultural traits and a high level of interaction, are regarded as a cultural unit. Race and ethnicity often form the basis of hierarchical ranking and determine who gets various resources. A majority (or dominant) group is one that is advantaged and has superior resources and rights in a society, while a minority (or subordinate) group is one whose members, because of physical or cultural characteristics, are disadvantaged and subjected to unequal treatment by the dominant group.

Prejudice is a negative attitude based on preconceived notions about the members of selected racial and ethnic groups. In some cases, people may develop prejudice because they are frustrated in their efforts to achieve a highly desired goal and need a scapegoat to blame. Prejudice also results from social learning. Finally, some individuals have an authoritarian personality, which is characterized by excessive conformity and rigid stereotypical thinking. Prejudice is often measured as levels of comfort in various social distance scenarios.

Discrimination refers to the actions or practices of dominant group members that have a harmful impact on members of a subordinate group. Racism is an organized set of beliefs about the innate inferiority of some racial groups, combined with the power to transform these ideas into practices. Racism involves elements of prejudice, discrimination, ethnocentrism, and stereotyping and takes many different forms, including overt racism, polite racism, subliminal racism, and institutionalized racism.

Symbolic interactionists point out that contact between people from divergent groups should lead to favourable attitudes and behaviour when members of each group have equal status, pursue the same goals, cooperate with one another to achieve their goals, and receive positive feedback during interactions. Functionalist explanations provide a description of how some early white ethnic immigrants assimilated into the mainstream. Conflict theorists focus on economic stratification and access to power in their analysis of race and ethnic relations. Feminist perspectives highlight the effects of gendered racism—the interactive effect of racism and sexism in the exploitation of women of colour. Interestingly, postmodern perspectives view racial and ethnic identities as organized around social structures which are fixed and close such as nations, tribes, bands, and communities. Finally, critical race theory is based on the belief that racism is such an ingrained feature of North American society that it appears to be ordinary and natural to many people. The unique experiences of Aboriginal peoples, the Québécois, and Canada's immigrant population are discussed along with the increasing racial and ethnic diversity of Canada.

Key Terms

assimilation *(p. 310)*

authoritarian personality *(p. 303)*

discrimination *(p. 303)*

ethnic group *(p. 299)*

ethnic pluralism *(p. 310)*

ethnocentrism *(p. 302)*

genocide *(p. 306)*

institutionalized racism *(p. 307)*

internal colonialism *(pp. 311 – 12)*

majority (dominant) group *(p. 301)*

minority (subordinate) group *(p. 301)*

overt racism *(p. 306)*

polite racism *(p. 307)*

prejudice *(p. 302)*

race *(p. 299)*

racial prejudice *(p. 302)*

racism *(p. 306)*

scapegoat *(p. 303)*

segregation *(p. 311)*

social distance *(pp. 303 − 04)*

split labour market *(p. 312)*

stereotypes *(p. 302)*

subliminal racism *(p. 307)*

systemic racism *(p. 308)*

visible minority *(p. 301)*

Key Terms Quiz

Review of Key Terms − Fill In the Blanks

1. _____ is a category of people who have been singled out as inferior or superior, often on the basis of real or alleged physical characteristics such as skin colour, hair texture, eye shape, or other subjectively selected attributes.

2. _____ is a person or group that is incapable of offering resistance to the hostility or aggression of others.

3. _____ is a process by which members of a subordinate racial or ethnic group become absorbed into the dominant culture.

4. _____ _____ is an attempt to disguise a dislike of others through behaviour that outwardly is nonprejudicial.

5. _____ _____ is characterized by excessive conformity, submissiveness to authority, intolerance, insecurity, a high level of superstition, and rigid, stereotypical thinking.

6. _____ is a negative attitude based on preconceived notions about members of selected groups.

7. _____ _____ is made up of the rules, procedures, and practices that directly and deliberately prevent minorities from having full and equal involvement in society.

8. _____ involves actions or practices of dominant group members (or their representatives) that have a harmful impact on members of a subordinate group.

9. _____ is the tendency to regard one's own culture and group as the standard, and thus superior, whereas all other groups are seen as inferior.

10. _____ _____ is a collection of people distinguished, by others or by themselves, primarily on the basis of cultural or nationality characteristics.

11. _____ _____ is the coexistence of a variety of distinct racial and ethnic groups within one society.

12. _____ _____ is a situation in which members of a racial or ethnic group are conquered or colonized and forcibly placed under the economic and political control of the dominant group.

13. _____ _____ _____ refers to the division of the economy into two areas of employment: a primary sector or upper tier, composed of higher-paid (usually dominant group) workers in more secure jobs, and a secondary sector or lower tier, made up of lower-paid (often subordinate group) workers in jobs with little security and hazardous working conditions.

14. _____ _____ is the extent to which people are willing to interact and establish relationships with members of racial and ethnic groups other than their own.

15. _____ is the spatial and social separation of categories of people by race, ethnicity, class, gender, and/or religion.

16. _____ _____ is a group that is advantaged and has superior resources and rights in a society.

17. _____ _____ is a group whose members, because of physical or cultural characteristics, are disadvantaged and subjected to unequal treatment by the dominant group and who regard themselves as objects of collective discrimination.

18. _____ _____ involves an unconscious criticism of minorities.

19. _____ _____ is a term for the practices, rules, and procedures of social institutions that have the unintended consequences of excluding minority group members.

20. _____ is a term for overgeneralizations about the appearance, behaviour, or other characteristics of members of particular groups.

21. _____ is a set of ideas that implies the superiority of one social group over another on the basis of biological or cultural characteristics, together with the power to put these beliefs into practice in a way that denies or excludes minority women and men.

22. _____ _____ is an official government category of nonwhite non-Caucasian individuals.

23. _____ is the deliberate, systematic killing of an entire people or nation.

24. _____ _____ is racism that takes the form of public statements about the "inferiority" of members of a racial or ethnic group.

25. _____ _____ is a term for beliefs that certain racial groups are innately inferior to others or have a disproportionate number of negative traits.

Key People

Emory Bogardus *(p. 303)*
Augie Fleras and Jean Leonard Elliott *(p. 299)*
Robert Merton *(p. 305)*

John Porter *(p. 300)*
Adrienne Shadd *(p. 311)*

Key People Quiz

Review of Key People – Matching Quiz

1. _____ Developed the concept of social distance to measure levels of prejudice.
2. _____ Described Canada as a "vertical mosaic."
3. _____ Developed a typology of prejudice and discriminatory types.
4. _____ Described segregation of Blacks in northern Ontario.
5. _____ Described the significance of "white privilege."

a. Emory Bogardus
b. Augie Fleras and Jean Leonard Elliott
c. Robert Merton
d. John Porter
e. Adrienne Shadd

Learning Objectives

After reading Chapter 10, the student should be able to:

1. define race and ethnic group and explain their social significance (pp. 299–301).
2. explain the sociological usage of the terms "majority group" and "minority group" and note why these terms may be misleading (p. 301).
3. define prejudice and explain how prejudice has its roots in stereotypes and ethnocentrism (pp. 302–03).
4. outline the scapegoat and authoritarian personality theories of prejudice (p. 303).

5. note how prejudice is measured (p. 305).

6. define discrimination, distinguish between *de jure* and *de facto* discrimination, and be familiar with the forms of discrimination identified by Robert Merton (pp. 303–06).

7. define racism and distinguish between overt racism, polite racism, subliminal racism, and systemic racism (pp. 306–08).

8. explain what the contact hypothesis refers to, and list the factors that must be present for interaction to produce favourable attitudes according to this hypothesis (pp. 308–10).

9. define assimilation and discuss how assimilation occurs at several distinct levels (p. 310).

10. define ethnic pluralism and note whether ethnic pluralism exists in Canada (pp. 310–11).

11. define segregation and explain the significance of the Jim Crow laws in the southern United States (p. 311).

12. define internal colonialism and note how experiences of internally colonized people are unique (pp. 311–12).

13. define split-labour-market theory (p. 312).

14. explain what is meant by "gendered racism" (pp. 312–13).

15. discuss how postmodern perspectives view ethnic and racial identities (pp. 313–14).

16. outline the major premises of critical race theory (p. 314).

17. explain how the experiences of Aboriginal peoples have been different from those of other racial and ethnic groups in Canada (pp. 315–17).

18. describe how the French Canadian experience in Canada has been unique when compared with other groups (pp. 317–18).

19. compare and contrast the experiences of Chinese, Japanese, South Asian, and Jewish Canadians (pp. 318–20).

20. discuss the prospects for growing racial and ethnic diversity in Canada (pp. 321–22).

Unit Mastery Quizzes

Unit Mastery – Multiple Choice

1. Which of the following statements about Canada's Aboriginal peoples is CORRECT?
   a. Aboriginal peoples are the most advantaged racial and ethnic group in Canada.
   b. Aboriginal peoples constitute an extremely homogenous group.
   c. Aboriginal peoples have been victims of genocide and forced migration.
   d. The Indian Act of 1876 protected the values, customs, and languages of Native people.

2. Which perspective uses a contact hypothesis to explain how interactions between people from divergent groups can lead to favourable attitudes and behaviour?
   a. symbolic interactionist
   b. functionalist
   c. conflict
   d. feminist

3. Beliefs that certain racial groups are innately inferior to others form the basis of:
   a. ethnocentrism.
   b. racial prejudice.
   c. discrimination.
   d. none of the above.

4. _____ theorists use the term "internal colonialism" to refer to a situation in which members of a racial or ethnic group are conquered or colonized and forcibly placed under the economic and political control of the dominant group.
   a. Symbolic interactionist
   b. Functionalist
   c. Conflict
   d. Feminist

5. Which of the following statements concerning French Canadians is FALSE?
   a. The British North America Act formally acknowledged the rights and privileges of the French and British as the founding groups of Canadian society.
   b. The French conquered the British in the Seven Years' War, rendering Canada a French dominion.
   c. In the 1960s Quebec nationalism grew and francophones in Quebec began to believe that their language and culture were threatened.
   d. Today approximately 23 percent of the Canadian population is francophone.

6. A(n) _____ group is defined by shared cultural traits and social interaction.
   a. racial
   b. ethnic
   c. majority
   d. minority

7. All of the following are considered a minority group in Canada EXCEPT:
   a. Chinese.
   b. white women.
   c. South Asians.
   d. all of the choices are considered minority members.

8. This perspective examines assimilation and pluralism as means for becoming part of a dominant group in society.
   a. symbolic interactionist
   b. functionalist
   c. conflict
   d. feminist

9. Which of the following statements about Canada's immigrants is FALSE?
   a. Chinese immigrants did not experience prejudice because they were recruited to work on the railway.
   b. Jewish Canadians today have a considerably higher level of education and income relative to the average Canadian.
   c. During World War II, people of Japanese ancestry were placed in internment camps because they were seen as a security threat.
   d. South Asians were denied citizenship and the right to vote in British Columbia until 1947.

10. In Nova Scotia, New Brunswick, and Ontario, Blacks were once set apart from Whites, which resulted in unequal access to power and privilege in schools, government, and the workplace. This is called:
   a. structural assimilation.
   b. cultural assimilation.
   c. ethnic pluralism.
   d. segregation.

11. All of the following are major patterns of interaction between racial and ethnic groups EXCEPT:
   a. assimilation.
   b. ethnic pluralism.
   c. social learning.
   d. internal colonization.

12. All of the following are patterns of interaction that develop between racial and ethnic groups EXCEPT:
   a. assimilation.
   b. immigration.
   c. ethnic pluralism.
   d. internal colonialism.

13. What type of discrimination is backed by explicit laws?
   a. overt racism
   b. institutionalized racism
   c. *de facto* discrimination
   d. *de jure* discrimination

14. According to this perspective, white workers in the upper tier of the employment sector use racial discrimination against nonwhites to protect their positions.
   a. authoritarian personality theory
   b. split-labour-market theory
   c. *de jure* discrimination
   d. internal colonialization

15. A situation in which many groups share elements of the mainstream culture while remaining culturally distinct from the dominant group is:
   a. apartheid.
   b. cultural assimilation.
   c. ethnic pluralism.
   d. internal colonialism.

16. An ethnic group shares all of the following EXCEPT:
    a. unique cultural traits.
    b. a sense of community.
    c. physical characteristics.
    d. ascribed membership from birth.

17. An ethnic group adopts the language, dress, values, and religion of the dominant group. This is an example of:
    a. structural assimilation.
    b. acculturation.
    c. amalgamation.
    d. psychological assimilation.

18. _____ occurs when members of subordinate racial or ethnic groups gain acceptance in everyday social interactions with members of the dominant group.
    a. Structural assimilation
    b. Biological assimilation
    c. Psychological assimilation
    d. Cultural assimilation

19. According to Merton's typology of prejudice and discrimination, a prejudiced discriminator:
    a. has a prejudiced attitude and acts in a discriminatory fashion.
    b. does not have a prejudiced attitude but acts in a discriminatory fashion.
    c. has a prejudiced attitude but does not act in a discriminatory fashion.
    d. does not have a prejudiced attitude and does not act in a discriminatory fashion.

20. Which perspective is most likely to claim that laws may remedy overt discrimination but have very little effect on subtle racism?
    a. critical race theory
    b. postmodern
    c. feminist
    d. interactionist

Unit Mastery – True or False

1. Race refers to physical and cultural features (p. 299).
   TRUE or FALSE

2. There is a significant degree of ethnic stratification in Canadian society (p. 301).
   TRUE or FALSE

3. A minority group has superior resources and rights in a society (p. 301).
   TRUE or FALSE

4. Affirmative action programs directed at hiring visible minorities are a form of reverse discrimination (pp. 299–300).
   TRUE or FALSE

5. To some extent, all people have prejudiced feelings against members of other groups (p. 302).
    TRUE or FALSE

6. Discrimination involves differential treatment based on irrelevant characteristics such as skin colour or language preference (pp. 303–04).
    TRUE or FALSE

7. For many Canadians, the media is a primary source of information about racial and ethnic groups (box, p. 304).
    TRUE or FALSE

8. Polite racism involves unconscious criticism of minorities (p. 307).
    TRUE or FALSE

9. Overt racism is conscious, personal, and explicit (p. 306).
    TRUE or FALSE

10. Racism involves elements of prejudice, ethnocentrism, stereotyping, and discrimination (p. 306).
    TRUE or FALSE

Unit Mastery − Fill In the Blanks

1. Enjoying the benefits that go along with being part of the dominant white group has been referred to as the _____ _____ (p. 300).

2. The term _____ _____ refers to an official government category of nonwhite non-Caucasian individuals (p. 301).

3. _____ involves the evaluation of all groups and cultures in terms of one's own cultural standards and values (p. 302).

4. _____ _____ takes the form of public statements about the "inferiority" of members of a racial or ethnic group (p. 306).

5. _____ _____ is not directly expressed, but is demonstrated in opposition to progressive minority policies (p. 307).

6. _____ _____ is entrenched in the structure, function, and processes of many social institutions (p. 308).

7. According to the split-labour-market theory, white workers in the _____ _____ may use racial discrimination against nonwhite workers to protect their positions (p. 312).

8. _____ _____ occurs when members of an ethnic group adopt dominant group traits, such as language or dress (p. 310).

9. _____ _____ occurs when members of subordinate racial or ethnic groups gain acceptance in everyday social interaction with members of the dominant group (p. 310).

10. _____ exists when specific ethnic groups are set apart from the dominant groups and have unequal access to power and privilege (p. 311).

Unit Mastery − Matching Quiz 1

Match the theory of prejudice with its key assumption:

1. _____ coexistence of many ethnic groups   a. assimilation
2. _____ conquering of racial or ethnic groups   b. ethnic pluralism
3. _____ spatial and social separation of   c. segregation
   categories   d. internal colonialism
4. _____ absorption of subordinate groups

Unit Mastery − Matching Quiz 2

Match the type of racism with its primary characteristic:

1. _____ unintentional and impersonal   a. overt racism
2. _____ deliberate and blatant   b. polite racism
3. _____ ambivalent and oblique   c. subliminal racism
4. _____ conscious and personal   d. institutional racism
5. _____ moderate and discreet   e. systemic racism

Solutions

Key Terms Quiz

Review of Key Terms − Fill In the Blanks

1. Race
2. Scapegoat
3. Assimilation
4. Polite racism
5. Authoritarian personality
6. Prejudice
7. Institutionalized racism
8. Discrimination
9. Ethnocentrism
10. Ethnic group
11. Ethnic pluralism
12. Internal colonialism
13. Split labour market
14. Social distance
15. Segregation
16. Majority group
17. Minority group
18. Subliminal racism
19. Systemic racism
20. Stereotype
21. Racism
22. Visible minority
23. Genocide
24. Overt racism
25. Racial prejudice

Key People Quiz

Review of Key People − Matching Quiz

1. A
2. D
3. C
4. E
5. B

Unit Mastery Quizzes

Unit Mastery − Multiple Choice

1. C
2. A
3. B
4. C
5. B
6. B
7. D
8. B
9. A
10. D
11. C
12. B
13. D
14. B
15. C
16. C
17. B
18. A
19. A
20. A

Unit Mastery − True or False

1. F, Race is a category of people who have been singled out as inferior or superior, often on the basis of real or alleged physical characteristics.
2. T
3. F, A minority group is one whose members, because of physical or cultural characteristics, are disadvantaged and subject to unequal treatment.
4. F, Affirmative action programs are efforts at eliminating disproportionate representation

that is often the end result of previous systemic racism.

5. T
6. T
7. T
8. F, Polite racism is an attempt to disguise a dislike of others through behaviour that outwardly is nonprejudicial. It includes a moderate degree of intent.
9. T
10. T

Unit Mastery − Fill In the Blanks

1. white privilege
2. visible minority
3. Ethnocentrism
4. Overt racism
5. Subliminal racism
6. Systemic racism
7. upper tier
8. Cultural assimilation
9. Structural assimilation
10. Segregation

Unit Mastery − Matching Quiz 1

1. B
2. D
3. C
4. A

Unit Mastery − Matching Quiz 2

1. E
2. D
3. C
4. A
5. B

Sex and Gender

Chapter Outline

Chapter Summary

It is important to distinguish between sex—the biological and anatomical differences between females and males—and gender—the socially constructed differences between females and males found in the meanings, beliefs, and practices associated with "femininity" and "masculinity." Sexism is the subordination of one sex (usually female), based on the superiority of the other sex. The differential treatment of women and men is linked to patriarchy, a hierarchical system in which cultural, political, and economic structures are dominated by men. In industrialized societies, a gap exists between unpaid work performed by women at home and paid work performed by men and unmarried women. In postindustrialized societies, women are double-burdened by employment in conjunction with familial responsibilities despite labour-saving devices in the form of technology.

The key agents of gender socialization are parents, peers, teachers and schools, sports, and the mass media, all of which tend to reinforce gender stereotypes. Gender inequality results from the economic, political, and educational discrimination of women. In most workplaces, either jobs are gender-segregated or the majority of employees are of the same gender. Even when women are employed in the same job as men, on average they do not receive the same, or equitable, pay. According to functional analysts, husbands perform instrumental tasks of economic support and decision making, and wives assume expressive tasks of providing affection and emotional support for the family. Conflict theorists suggest that the gendered division of labour within families and the workplace results from male control and dominance over women and resources. Feminist perspectives contend that women and men are equal and therefore advocate social change to eradicate gender inequality. Although the pay gap between men and women will continue to shrink the future, many gender issues are likely to remain unresolved.

Key Terms

body consciousness *(p. 333)*

discourses *(p. 356)*

employment equity *(p. 350)*

feminism *(p. 355)*

gender *(pp. 332 – 33)*

gender bias *(p. 343)*

gender identity *(p. 333)*

gender role *(p. 333)*

hermaphrodite *(p. 330)*

homophobia *(p. 332)*

matriarchy *(p. 335*

patriarchy *(p. 335)*

pay equity (comparable worth) *(p. 350)*

primary sex characteristics *(p. 329)*

secondary sex characteristics *(p. 329)*
sex *(p. 329)*
sexism *(p. 334)*
sexual orientation *(p. 331)*

transsexual *(p. 330)*
transvestite *(p. 330)*
wage gap *(p. 349)*

Key Terms Quiz

Review of Key Terms – Fill In the Blanks

1. _____ is extreme prejudice directed against gays, lesbians, bisexuals, and others who are perceived as not being heterosexual.

2. _____ is the belief that women and men are equal and that they should be valued equally and have equal rights.

3. _____ is the term used for the biological and anatomical differences between females and males.

4. _____ is the subordination of one sex, usually female, based on the assumed superiority of the other sex.

5. _____ is a person who believes that he or she was born with the body of the wrong sex.

6. _____ _____ consists of showing favouritism toward one gender over another.

7. _____ is a hierarchical system of social organization in which cultural, political, and economic structures are controlled by men.

8. _____ is a hierarchical system of social organization in which cultural, political, and economic structures are controlled by women.

9. _____ is a person in whom sexual differentiation is ambiguous or incomplete.

10. _____ _____ is how a person perceives and feels about his or her body; it also includes an awareness of social conditions in society that contribute to this self-knowledge.

11. _____ refers to the culturally and socially constructed differences between females and males found in the meanings, beliefs, and practices associated with "femininity" and "masculinity."

12. _____ _____ refers to the attitudes, behaviour, and activities that are socially defined as appropriate for each sex and are learned through the socialization process.

13. _____ _____ is a person's perception of the self as female or male.

14. _____ _____ is a preference for emotional–sexual relationships with members of the opposite sex (heterosexuality), the same sex (homosexuality), or both sexes (bisexuality).

15. _____ is a male who lives as a woman or a female who lives as a man but does not alter the genitalia.

16. _____ _____ characteristics are the genitalia used in the reproductive process.

17. _____ _____ characteristics are the physical traits (other than reproductive organs) that identify an individual's sex.

18. _____ _____ is a term used to describe the disparity between women's and men's earnings.

19. _____ _____ is a strategy to eliminate the effects of discrimination and to fully open the competition for job opportunities to those who have been excluded historically.

20. _____ _____ is a term that reflects the belief that wages ought to reflect the worth of a job, not the gender or race of the worker.

Key People

Ben Agger *(p. 355)*

George F. Gilder *(p. 353)*

Dorothy C. Holland and Margaret A. Eisenhart *(p. 342)*

Judith Lorber *(p. 347)*

Michael A. Messner *(p. 345)*

Myra Sadker and David Sadker *(p. 343)*

Key People Quiz

Review of Key People – Matching Quiz

1. _____ Claimed that girls and women have been empowered by their entry into sports; however, sex segregation of female and male athletes, as well as coaches, persists.
2. _____ Claimed that men can be feminists and propose feminist theories.
3. _____ Argued that traditional gender roles are important for individuals and for the economic and social order of society.
4. _____ Found that the peer system propelled women into a world of romance in which their attractiveness to men counted most.
5. _____ Found that teachers consistently devote more time to boys and to girls.
6. _____ Notes how in most industrialized countries, jobs are segregated by gender and race/ethnicity.

a. Ben Agger
b. George F. Gilder
c. Dorothy C. Holland and Margaret A. Eisenhart
d. Michael A. Messner
e. Myra Sadker and David Sadker
f. Judith Lorber

Learning Objectives

After reading Chapter 11, the student should be able to:

1. define sex and distinguish between primary and secondary sex characteristics (p. 329).
2. explain why sex is not always clear-cut and differentiate between hermaphrodites, transsexuals, and transvestites (p. 330).
3. define sexual orientation and note the criteria used by social scientists to classify individuals as gay, lesbian, or bisexual. (pp. 331–32).
4. define gender and explain its social significance (pp. 332–34).
5. describe the relationship between gender roles and gender identity (p. 333).
6. explain how body consciousness is related to gender identity and describe how eating disorders and bodybuilding illustrate the social significance of gender (pp. 333–34).
7. define sexism and explain how it is related to patriarchy (pp. 334–35).
8. explain how gender stratification in hunting and gathering societies differs from that in horticultural and pastoral societies (pp. 335–36).
9. outline the similarities and differences in gender stratification between agrarian, industrial, and postindustrial societies (pp. 336–39).

10. describe the process of gender socialization and identify specific ways in which parents and peers contribute to this process (pp. 339–43).

11. describe gender bias and explain how schools operate as a gendered institution (pp. 343–44).

12. describe the relationship between sports and gender socialization (pp. 344–46).

13. explain how the mass media contribute to gender socialization (pp. 346–47).

14. discuss the gendered segregation of paid work (pp. 346–49).

15. explain what pay equity is and how you determine if pay discrimination exists (p. 350).

16. trace changes in the labour force participation by women and note how these changes have contributed to a "second shift" (pp. 351–52).

17. describe functionalist and neoclassical economic perspectives (pp. 353–54).

18. note how conflict theorists view gender stratification (p. 354).

19. outline the key assumptions of liberal, radical, socialist, multicultural, and postmodern feminism (pp. 355–57).

20. outline key assumptions of symbolic interactionist perspectives (pp. 357–58).

Unit Mastery Quizzes

Unit Mastery – Multiple Choice

1. A hermaphrodite is a person who:
   a. believes that he or she was born with the body of the wrong sex.
   b. has a sexual preference for members of the opposite sex.
   c. has some combination of male and female genitals.
   d. behaves and dresses like a woman but is really a man.

2. Which of the following statements best explains the social significance of excessive dieting and bodybuilding?
   a. Compulsive dieting and bodybuilding results in the formation of hermaphrodites.
   b. Gender is absent from dieting and bodybuilding.
   c. Dieting and bodybuilding helps eliminate gender stereotypes.
   d. The body is objectified in both compulsive dieting and bodybuilding.

3. Which of the following statements accurately describes the similarity between agrarian and industrialized societies?
   a. Men control procreation and women's status is low.
   b. Women control procreation and women's status is high.
   c. Men and women have equal status and control over procreation.
   d. Inheritance is shared and women's status is high.

4. Which of the following statements about gender socialization is FALSE?
    a. From birth, parents act toward children on the basis of the child's sex.
    b. Peers help children learn prevailing gender stereotypes.
    c. Peers help children learn gender-inappropriate behaviour.
    d. Female peer groups put more pressure on girls to do feminine things than male peer groups place on boys to do masculine things.

5. Gender stereotyping through the mass media is evident in:
    a. the fact that all forms of advertising (whether on television, billboards, or in magazines) reinforce ideas about women and physical attractiveness.
    b. a high rate of lively adventure, noise, and violence on television because advertisers hope to appeal to boys, who constitute a significant portion of the viewing audience for some shows.
    c. the fact that male characters are more aggressive and direct, while female characters are seen as manipulating through displays of helplessness or seduction.
    d. all of the above are examples of mass media gender stereotyping.

6. Which of the following statements about the gendered division of paid work in Canada is FALSE?
    a. Women remain concentrated in lower-paying, traditionally female jobs.
    b. Women are severely underrepresented in the top Canadian corporations.
    c. There is no gender segregation in the workplace.
    d. Gender-segregated work has a negative effect on men and women.

7. All of the following are criticisms of functionalist perspectives on gender EXCEPT:
    a. Problems inherent in traditional gender roles, including the personal role strains of men and women, are minimized by this approach.
    b. The functionalist approach does not take a critical look at the structures of society that make educational and occupational opportunities more available to some than to others.
    c. The functionalist approach fails to examine the underlying power relations between men and women.
    d. All of the above are criticisms of the functionalist perspective.

8. All of the following are anticipated gender trends for the future EXCEPT:
    a. The pay gap between men and women should continue to decrease.
    b. Gender segregation may increase if the number of female-dominated jobs continues to grow.
    c. Many men will continue to join movements to raise consciousness about men's concerns.
    d. Affirmative action programs will be prohibited.

9. Biological attributes of men and women are referred to as:
    a. gender.
    b. sex.
    c. sexual orientation.
    d. sexism.

10. Social and cultural processes, not biological "givens," are most important in defining what females and males are and what they should do. This argument favours:
   a. gender.
   b. sex.
   c. sexual orientation.
   d. sexism.

11. Being small and weak as a male often results in disapproval of others. This illustrates:
   a. patriarchy.
   b. sexism.
   c. sexual orientation.
   d. body consciousness.

12. Which of the following statements about horticultural and pastoral societies is TRUE?
   a. Inheritance is patrilineal.
   b. Women's status is very low.
   c. Men own the means of production and control procreation.
   d. Men begin to control societies and women's status starts to decrease.

13. In which form of feminism is gender equality equated with equality of opportunity?
   a. radical feminism
   b. liberal feminism
   c. socialist feminism
   d. multicultural feminism

14. The term "second shift" is generally used to refer to:
   a. additional unpaid hours worked by employees who have little job security.
   b. having to work a part-time job along with a full-time one to make ends meet.
   c. the dual responsibilities that females face in terms of paid employment in conjunction with child care and housework.
   d. time segregation in the workplace.

15. The belief that wages ought to reflect the worth of a job, not the gender or race of the worker is known as:
   a. pay equity.
   b. wage gap.
   c. sexism.
   d. employment equity.

16. Which of the following statements about sports and gender socialization is FALSE?
   a. Boys are socialized to participate in highly competitive, rule-oriented games.
   b. For females, being an athlete and a woman may constitute contradictory statuses.
   c. For males, competitive sport becomes a means of constructing a masculine identity, a legitimated outlet for violence and aggression, and an avenue for upward mobility.
   d. Few college and professional sports are sex-segregated today.

17. Sexism directed at women contains all of the following elements EXCEPT:
    a. negative attitudes toward women.
    b. stereotypical beliefs that reinforce, complement, or justify the prejudice.
    c. sexual orientation.
    d. discrimination.

18. Which of the following statements about gender identity is FALSE?
    a. Gender identity concerns one's perception of the self as a male or female.
    b. Gender identity is established by the time a person reaches three years of age.
    c. Gender identity includes behaviours and activities that are socially defined as appropriate for each sex.
    d. Most people form a gender identification that matches their biological sex.

19. Which of the following statements about gender socialization by teachers and schools is FALSE?
    a. Most fields of study retain a male or female orientation.
    b. Teacher–student interactions influence not only students' learning but also their self-esteem.
    c. Studies show that one of the messages that teachers may communicate is that girls are more important than boys.
    d. The content of teacher–student interaction is very important.

20. Which perspective argues that traditional gender roles are important not only for individuals but also for the economic and social order of society?
    a. feminist
    b. functionalist
    c. human capital model
    d. postmodern

Unit Mastery – True or False

1. At birth, male and female infants are distinguished by secondary sex characteristics (p. 329).
   TRUE or FALSE

2. Western societies acknowledge the existence of only two sexes (p. 330).
   TRUE or FALSE

3. Body consciousness is a part of gender identity (p. 333).
   TRUE or FALSE

4. A transsexual believes that he or she was born with the body of the wrong sex (p. 330).
   TRUE or FALSE

5. The earliest known division of labour between women and men is in hunting and gathering societies (p. 335).
   TRUE or FALSE

6. Occupational gender segregation contributes to stratification in society (p. 349).
   TRUE or FALSE

7. At conception, the father contributes an X chromosome and the mother either an X or Y chromosome (p. 329).
    TRUE or FALSE

8. Gender identity is typically established between eighteen months and three years of age (p. 333).
    TRUE or FALSE

9. Gender-segregated work is most visible in occupations that remain more than 90 percent female (i.e., secretary and registered nurse) (p. 348).
    TRUE or FALSE

10. According to radical feminists, male domination causes all forms of human oppression (p. 355).
    TRUE or FALSE

Unit Mastery − Fill In the Blanks

1. At puberty, an increased production of hormones results in the development of _____ _____ _____ (p. 329).

2. _____ tend to have some combination of male and female genitalia (p. 330).

3. A _____ is genetically of one sex but has a gender identity of the other sex (p. 330).

4. The term _____ was created to describe individuals whose appearance, behaviour, or self-identification does not conform to the common social rules of gender expression (p. 332).

5. _____ _____ or comparable worth is the idea that wages should correspond to the worth of a job, not the gender of the worker (p. 350).

6. In Canadian society, males are expected to demonstrate aggressiveness and toughness as part of their _____ _____ (p. 333).

7. The word _____ is often used to refer to the biological attributes of men and women (p. 329).

8. _____ _____ strategies focus on ways to move women into higher-paying jobs through recruitment, selection, training, development, and promotion (p. 350).

9. The _____ perspective views men and women as having distinct roles that are important for the survival of the family and society (p. 353).

10. According to _____ feminists, women's oppression results from their dual roles as paid and unpaid workers in a capitalist economy (p. 355).

Unit Mastery − Matching Quiz 1

Match the type of society to its key feature:

1. __c__ Male dominance is promoted by practices such as menstrual taboos, bridewealth, and polygyny.
2. __a__ Gender equality exists because neither sex has the ability to provide all of the food necessary for survival.
3. __b__ *Purdah*, footbinding, and genital mutilation lower women's status.
4. __d__ Factory or mechanized production replaces agriculture and women's status further declines.
5. __e__ Technology supports a service and information-based economy and education becomes crucial for the success of men and women.

a. hunting and gathering
b. horticultural and pastoral
c. agrarian
d. industrial
e. postindustrial

Unit Mastery − Matching Quiz 2

Match the gender socialization agent with its key attribute:

1. _____ Devote more time, effort, and attention to boys than girls.
2. __a__ Encourage males to be highly competitive.
3. __a__ Purchase clothing and toys that reflect gender expectations.
4. __b__ Are most influential during adolescence.
5. __e__ Reinforce the notion that women can never be too young or too thin.

a. parents
b. peers
c. teachers
d. sports
e. mass media

Unit Mastery − Matching Quiz 3

Match the theoretical perspective to its key argument:

1. _____ What individuals earn is the result of their own choices and labour market needs.
2. _____ The gendered division of labour within families and the workplace results from male control of and dominance over women and resources.
3. _____ A husband should perform the instrumental tasks and a wife should perform the expressive ones.
4. _____ Women's oppression results from their dual roles as paid and unpaid workers.
5. _____ Gender equality is equated with equality of opportunity.
6. _____ Male domination causes all forms of human oppression, including racism and classism.
7. _____ Women of colour experience a different world than middle-class white women because of multilayered oppression.
8. _____ View discourses as constructs of social reality and consider discourses to be mechanisms of social control.

a. functionalist
b. human capital model
c. conflict
d. liberal feminism
e. radical feminism
f. socialist feminism
g. postmodern feminism
h. multicultural feminism

Solutions

Key Terms Quiz

Review of Key Terms – Fill In the Blanks

1. Homophobia
2. Feminism
3. Sex
4. Sexism
5. Transsexual
6. Gender bias
7. Patriarchy
8. Matriarchy
9. Hermaphrodite
10. Body consciousness
11. Gender
12. Gender role
13. Gender identity
14. Sexual orientation
15. Transvestite
16. Primary sex
17. Secondary sex
18. Wage gap
19. Employment equity
20. Pay equity

Key People Quiz

Review of Key People – Matching Quiz

1. D
2. A
3. B
4. C
5. E
6. F

Unit Mastery Quizzes

Unit Mastery – Multiple Choice

1. C
2. D
3. A
4. D
5. D
6. C
7. D
8. D
9. B
10. A
11. D
12. D
13. B
14. C
15. A
16. D
17. C
18. C
19. C
20. B

Unit Mastery – True or False

1. F, At birth, male and female infants are distinguished by primary sex characteristics.
2. T
3. T
4. T
5. T
6. T
7. F, At conception, the mother contributes the X chromosome, and the father determines the sex of the embryo via an X or Y chromosome.
8. T
9. T
10. T

Unit Mastery – Fill In the Blanks

1. secondary sex characteristics
2. Hermaphrodites
3. transsexual
4. transgender
5. Pay equity
6. gender role
7. sex
8. Employment equity
9. functionalist
10. socialist

Unit Mastery – Matching Quiz 1

1. B
2. A
3. C
4. D
5. E

Unit Mastery – Matching Quiz 2

1. C
2. D
3. A
4. B
5. E

Unit Mastery – Matching Quiz 3

1. B
2. C
3. A
4. F
5. D
6. E
7. H
8. G

Aging

Chapter Outline

Chapter Summary

Aging includes the physical, psychological, and social processes associated with growing older. In Canada, the proportion of people age 65 and older is increasing, while the young are decreasing. In preindustrial societies, people of all ages are expected to work, and the contributions of older people are valued. In industrialized societies, older people are expected to retire so that younger people may take their place. In North America, age differentiation is based on narrowly defined categories such as middle adulthood and later adulthood. Age differentiation in Canada produces inequalities, differences, segregation, or conflict between age groups. Ageism—prejudice and discrimination against people on the basis of age—is reinforced by stereotypes of older people. Elder abuse includes physical, psychological, and medical abuse, and financial exploitation of people age 65 or older.

Functionalist explanations such as disengagement theory focus on how older persons adjust to their changing roles in society. Activity theory, an interactionist perspective, states that people change in late middle age and find substitutes for previous statuses, roles, and activities. Conflict theorists link the loss of status and power to a lack of ability to produce and maintain wealth. Feminists point out that women are much more likely to be poor in old age. Postmodern perspectives note how older people can experiment with new identities and find assistance in anti-aging technologies.

Support services and homemaker services provide less expensive alternatives to daycare (institutionalization) for older persons. As we look to the future, it is important to note that most of the population growth will take place in the older age cohorts, placing a greater demand on social resources and programs that provide support to the elderly.

Key Terms

activity theory *(p. 381)*

ageism *(p. 375)*

age stratification *(p. 369)*

aging *(p. 364)*

chronological age *(p. 364)*

cohort *(p. 367)*

disengagement theory *(p. 380)*

elder abuse *(p. 379)*

functional age *(p. 364)*

hospice *(p. 390)*

life expectancy *(p. 367)*

social gerontology *(p. 367)*

Key Terms Quiz

Review of Key Terms – Fill In the Blanks

1. _____ _____ is a person's age based on date of birth.

2. _____ _____ is physical abuse, psychological abuse, financial exploitation, and medical abuse or neglect of people age 65 and older.

3. _____ _____ involves observerable individual attributes such as physical appearance, mobility, strength, coordination, and mental capacity that are used to assign people to age categories.

4. _____ _____ states that people tend to shift gears in late middle age and find substitutes for previous statuses, roles, and activities.

5. _____ is a group of people born within a specified period of time.

6. _____ is prejudice and discrimination against people on the basis of age, particularly when they are older persons.

7. _____ is the physical, psychological, and social processes associated with growing older.

8. _____ is a homelike facility that provides supportive care for patients with terminal illnesses.

9. _____ _____ is the study of the social (nonphysical) aspects of aging.

10. _____ _____ is the inequalities, differences, segregation, or conflict between age groups.

11. _____ _____ claims that older persons make a normal and healthy adjustment to aging when they detach themselves from their social roles and prepare for eventual death.

12. _____ _____ is the average length of time a group of individuals of the same age will live.

Key People

Elaine C. Cumming and William E. Henry *(p. 380)*

Anne Fausto-Sterling *(p. 370)*

Melissa A. Hardy and Lawrence E. Hazelrigg *(p. 385)*

Elisabeth Kübler-Ross *(p. 389)*

William C. Levin *(p. 376)*

Patricia Moore *(p. 377)*

Key People Quiz

Review of Key People – Matching Quiz

1. _____ Studied the experience of menopause during middle adulthood and concluded that many women respond negatively to menopause because of negative stereotypes associated with menopausal and postmenopausal women.

2. _____ Found that gender was more directly related to poverty in older persons than was ethnicity, educational background, or occupational status.

3. _____ At age 27, disguised herself as an 85-year-old woman to study how people respond to age.

4. _____ Coined the term "disengagement theory" and noted that disengagement can be functional both for the individual and for society.

5. _____ Outlined five stages people use in coping with death: denial, anger, bargaining, depression, and acceptance.

6. _____ Found that college students rated a 73-year-old man in photographs as less competent, less intelligent, and less reliable than photographed men who were 25 and 52 years old.

a. Elaine C. Cumming and William E. Henry
b. Anne Fausto-Sterling
c. Melissa A. Hardy and Lawrence E. Hazelrigg
d. Elisabeth Kübler-Ross
e. William C. Levin
f. Patricia Moore

Learning Objectives

After reading Chapter 12, the student should be able to:

1. define aging (p. 364).

2. differentiate between chronological age and functional age and note the social significance of each (pp. 364–65).

3. trace recent trends in aging and explain how life expectancy has changed in Canada during the twentieth century (pp. 365–67).

4. define cohort and explain how cohorts help establish population trends (p. 367).

5. explain how historical perspectives on age differ from contemporary ones (pp. 367–68).

6. list the two key age strata discussed in this chapter and note a key feature of each in North America (pp. 369–75).

7. discuss retirement in Canada and how pension relates to this concept (pp. 372–75).

8. discuss ageism and describe the negative stereotypes associated with older persons (pp. 375–77).

9. describe how older people as a group have fared economically in recent decades (pp. 377–79).

10. note how political change in Russia has had an impact on the structure of the Russian population (pp. 378–79).

11. define elder abuse (p. 379).

12. explain how functionalist perspectives view aging (pp. 380–81).

13. explain how symbolic interactionist perspectives view aging (pp. 381–83).

14. explain how conflict perspectives view aging (pp. 383–84).

15. explain why poverty in old age is largely a woman's problem (pp. 384–85).

16. outline how a postmodern perspective views aging (pp. 385–86).

17. be familiar with living arrangements for older adults (pp. 386–88).

18. note major changes in views on death and dying over time and describe some of the controversial issues surrounding death (pp. 388–90).

19. list and describe Elisabeth Kübler-Ross's five stages used to explain how people cope with the process of dying (p. 389).

20. describe some of the key trends in aging expected for the early decades of the twenty-first century and note the consequences of these trends (pp. 390–91).

Unit Mastery Quizzes

Unit Mastery – Multiple Choice

1. Age that is based on physical appearance, mental capacity, and strength is:
   a. functional.
   b. chronological.
   c. gerontological.
   d. cohort-based.

2. Which of the following statements contains the correct categories of late adulthood?
   a. young-old, middle-old, old-old
   b. young-old, old-old, oldest-old
   c. young-old, middle-old, late-old
   d. old-old, older-old, oldest-old

3. A cohort is defined as:
   a. a group of people born within a specified period of time.
   b. the average length of time a group of individuals of the same age will live.
   c. the number of persons of each age level within the society.
   d. observable individual attributes such as mobility and strength that are used to assign people to age categories.

4. Which statement best describes the economic situation of older people in Canada?
   a. The income of people over the age of 65 has deteriorated in the past ten years.
   b. Older people tend to have less wealth but more income than younger people.
   c. The income of people over the age of 65 has improved in the last two decades.
   d. Very few of Canada's older citizens are poor or near-poor.

5. In this stage of the life course, most people have their highest levels of income and prestige.
   a. adolescence
   b. young adulthood
   c. middle adulthood
   d. late adulthood

6. Which theory claims that people tend to find substitutes for previous statuses, roles, and activities in late middle age?
   a. stratification
   b. ageism
   c. disengagement
   d. activity

7. Which of the following statements about the elderly is FALSE?
   a. The rates of criminal victimization for seniors are lower than for their younger counterparts.
   b. The vast majority of abuse incidents are reported by elderly victims.
   c. Older people report more fear of crime relative to their younger counterparts.
   d. The consequences of victimization are more likely to be serious for an older person relative to a younger one.

8. Which of the following statements about living arrangements for older adults is FALSE?
   a. Nursing homes are the most restrictive environment for older persons.
   b. A decline in support services has led to an increase in the rate of institutionalization over the past three decades.
   c. Support services and day care for older persons are far less expensive than institutionalized care.
   d. Women are more likely to enter nursing homes because of their greater life expectancy, higher rates of chronic illness, and higher rates of widowhood.

9. All of the following are stages in coping with dying as identified by Elisabeth Kübler-Ross EXCEPT:
   a. resentment
   b. denial
   c. bargaining
   d. depression

10. Elder abuse consists of:
    a. physical and psychological abuse.
    b. medical abuse or neglect.
    c. financial exploitation.
    d. all of the above are forms of elder abuse.

11. In this stage of the life course, people experience secondary aging, which occurs as a result of environmental factors and lifestyle choices (e.g., smoking).
    a. adolescence
    b. young adulthood
    c. middle adulthood
    d. late adulthood

12. Which of the following statements about stages in the life course is TRUE?
    a. In middle adulthood men undergo a climacteric in which the production of testosterone decreases.
    b. People begin to experience senescence in late adulthood.
    c. People are expected to get married, have children, and secure a job during middle adulthood.
    d. Most women undergo menopause during late adulthood.

13. All of the following are key trends in aging in Canada EXCEPT:
    a. Today, about 12 percent of Canadians are 65 years of age or older.
    b. Canada's population is one of the oldest in the world.
    c. The aging of the Canadian population resulted from an increase in life expectancy combined with a decrease in birth rates.
    d. Males have a higher life expectancy at birth than their female counterparts.

14. Which of the following statements accurately depicts the role of age two hundred years ago?
    a. Older individuals played little or no role in food production.
    b. Older individuals were expected to retire while they were still physically able to work.
    c. Preteens and teenagers played little or no role in food production.
    d. Young persons were expected to act like adults and do adult work.

15. Which perspective focuses on how older persons adjust to their changing roles in society?
    a. functionalist
    b. interactionist
    c. conflict
    d. feminist

16. Conflict theorists view aging as especially problematic in contemporary capitalist societies because:
    a. people have trouble finding substitutes for previous statuses, roles, and activities.
    b. as people grow older, their power tends to diminish unless they are able to maintain wealth.
    c. people are unable to make normal and healthy adjustments to aging.
    d. none of the above.

17. Prejudice and discrimination directed at people on the basis of age is called:
    a. disengagement.
    b. hospice.
    c. ageism.
    d. gerontology.

18. Disengagement theory is part of which perspective on aging?
    a. interactionist
    b. conflict
    c. functionalist
    d. feminist

19. Which perspective claims that persons in positions of power create policies that keep people with disabilities in a subservient position?
    a. functionalist
    b. conflict
    c. interactionist
    d. postmodern

20. Which of the following statements highlights an important controversy surrounding death and dying?
    a. It is not clear whether parents of incompetent persons in permanent vegetative states have the legal right to refuse medical treatment.
    b. It is not clear whether individuals suffering from an incurable, terminal illness have the right to decide when their life should end.
    c. There is no national standard for determining when life support measures should be ended.
    d. All of the above are controversial issues that relate to death and dying.

Unit Mastery – True or False

1. Older persons may be viewed as incompetent solely on the basis of their age (p. 364).
   TRUE or FALSE

2. Today, older Canadians make up more than one-tenth of the population (p. 365).
   TRUE or FALSE

3. Since the beginning of the twentieth century, life expectancy has steadily decreased (p. 367).
   TRUE or FALSE

4. In North America, age differentiation is based on narrowly defined categories that have a profound effect on our perceptions of people's capabilities and entitlements (p. 369).
   TRUE or FALSE

5. Wrinkles and grey hair are visible signs of senescence (p. 369).
   TRUE or FALSE

6. Alzheimer's disease is an organic mental disorder that affects all age groups in the population (p. 370).
   TRUE or FALSE

7. Interactionist perspectives examine the connection between life satisfaction in a person's later years and an active lifestyle (p. 381).

   TRUE or FALSE

8. Currently, all working people in Canada are covered by the Canada or Quebec Pension Plans (p. 372).

   TRUE or FALSE

9. From an interactionist perspective, as people grow older, their power tends to diminish unless they are able to maintain wealth (p. 383).

   TRUE or FALSE

10. Pensions are one of the most important factors affecting retirement plans (p. 372).

   TRUE or FALSE

Unit Mastery − Fill In the Blanks

1. _____ _____ is the average length of time a group of individuals of the same age will live (p. 367).

2. _____ is the study of aging and older people (p. 367).

3. _____ _____ is the number of persons of each age level within the society (p. 367).

4. _____ against older persons is rooted in the assumption that people become unattractive, unintelligent, asexual, uemployable, and mentally incompetent as they grow older (p. 375).

5. _____ explanations of aging focus on how older persons adjust to their changing roles in society (p. 380).

6. When people say "Act your age," they are referring to _____ _____ , a person's age based on date of birth (p. 364).

7. Referred to as the _____ _____ _____ , the aging of the Canadian population resulted from an increase in life expectancy combined with a decrease in birth rates (p. 367).

8. A _____ is a homelike facility that provides supportive care for patients with terminal illnesses (p. 390).

9. _____ _____ are the most restrictive environments for older persons (p. 387).

10. Many people have chosen to have a say in how their own lives might end by signing a _____ _____ , which documents the circumstances under which their life should end (p. 389).

Unit Mastery – Matching Quiz 1

Match the theoretical perspective to its key concept:

1. _____ activity
2. _____ disengagement
3. _____ capitalism
4. _____ new identities
5. _____ feminization of poverty

a. functionalist
b. interactionist
c. conflict
d. feminist
e. postmodern

Unit Mastery – Matching Quiz 2

Match the age strata to its key feature:

1. _____ pension plans
2. _____ young-old and oldest-old
3. _____ menopause and climacteric

a. middle adulthood
b. late adulthood
c. retirement

Solutions

Key Terms Quiz

Review of Key Terms – Fill In the Blanks

1. Chronological age
2. Elder abuse
3. Functional age
4. Activity theory
5. Cohort
6. Ageism
7. Aging
8. Hospice
9. Social gerontology
10. Age stratification
11. Disengagement theory
12. Life expectancy

Key People Quiz

Review of Key People – Matching Quiz

1. B
2. C
3. F
4. A
5. D
6. E

Unit Mastery Quizzes

Unit Mastery – Multiple Choice

1. A
2. B
3. A
4. C
5. C
6. D
7. B
8. B
9. A
10. D
11. C
12. A
13. D
14. D
15. A
16. B
17. C
18. C
19. B
20. D

Unit Mastery – True or False

1. T
2. T
3. F, Since the beginning of the twentieth century, life expectancy has steadily increased as industrialized nations developed better water and sewage systems, improved nutrition, and made tremendous advances in medical science.
4. T
5. T
6. F, Alzheimer's is restricted to late adulthood and accounts for about 55 percent of all organic mental disorders in the older population.
7. T
8. T
9. F, From a conflict perspective, power diminishes, rendering aging as especially problematic in contemporary capitalist societies.
10. T

Unit Mastery – Fill In the Blanks

1. Life expectancy
2. Gerontology
3. Age structure
4. Ageism
5. Functionalist
6. chronological age
7. greying of Canada
8. hospice
9. Nursing homes
10. living will

Unit Mastery – Matching Quiz 1

1. B
2. A
3. C
4. E
5. D

Unit Mastery – Matching Quiz 2

1. C
2. B
3. A

The Economy and Work

Chapter Outline

Chapter Summary

The economy is the social institution that ensures the maintenance of society through the production, distribution, and consumption of goods and services. Preindustrial societies are characterized by primary sector production, in which workers extract raw materials and natural resources from the environment. Industrial societies engage in secondary sector production, which is based on the processing of raw materials into finished goods. Postindustrial societies involve the provision of services rather than goods. Capitalism involves private ownership of the means of production, pursuit of personal profit, competition, and lack of government intervention. Socialism is characterized by public ownership, collective goals, and centralized decision making. A mixed economy, sometimes referred to as democratic socialism, is a system that combines private ownership, governmental distribution of some essential goods and services, and free elections.

Functionalists view the economy as vital for the distribution of good and services while conflict theorists consider business cycles to be a function of capitalist greed. Symbolic interactionists tend to emphasize the meaning of work and job satisfaction as a source of self-identity. Feminists draw our attention to women's unpaid work in the home and gender inequality in wages.

Occupations are categories of jobs that involve similar activities at different work sites. Professions are high-status, knowledge-based occupations characterized by abstract, specialized knowledge, autonomy, and authority over clients. Marginal jobs violate employment norms such as adequate hours and pay. Contingent work is part-time work, temporary work, and subcontracted work. Unemployment remains a problem for many workers. In an effort to improve their work environment and gain some control over their own work-related activities through collective bargaining, some workers have joined labour unions.

As we move into a postindustrial economy, traditional jobs are falling victim to technology. In some cases, hours of work are increasing as high-level employees are now continuously connected to work through cellular phones, faxes, and computers. Canadian industry continues to compete with companies around the globe, while workers are increasingly fragmented into two major market divisions: (1) those who work in the innovative, primary sector and (2) those whose jobs are located in the growing marginal, secondary sector.

Key Terms

capitalism *(p. 402)*

contingent work *(p. 416)*

corporations *(p. 402)*

democratic socialism *(p. 406)*

economy *(p. 396)*

labour union *(p. 418)*

marginal jobs *(p. 415)*

mixed economy *(p. 406)*

multinational corporations *(p. 403)*

occupations *(p. 411)*

oligopoly *(p. 404)*

postindustrial economy *(p. 400)*

primary sector production *(p. 397)*

professions *(p. 412)*

secondary sector production *(p. 399)*

socialism *(p. 405)*

unemployment rate *(p. 418)*

Key Terms Quiz

Review of Key Terms – Fill In the Blanks

1. _____ _____ _____ is the extraction of raw materials and natural resources from the environment.

2. _____ _____ _____ is the processing of raw materials into finished goods.

3. _____ _____ is based on the provision of services rather than goods.

4. _____ exists when several companies overwhelmingly control an entire industry.

5. The _____ is the social institution that ensures the maintenance of society through the production, distribution, and consumption of goods and services.

6. _____ _____ are large companies that are headquartered in one country and have subsidiaries or branches in other countries.

7. _____ are high-status, knowledge-based occupations.

8. _____ are categories of jobs that involve similar activities at different work sites.

9. _____ is an economic system characterized by public ownership of the means of production, the pursuit of collective goals, and centralized decision making.

10. _____ is an economic system characterized by private ownership of the means of production, from which personal profits can be derived through market competition and without government intervention.

11. _____ are large-scale organizations that have legal powers, such as the ability to enter into contracts and buy and sell property, separately from their individual owners.

12. _____ _____ is an economic and political system that combines private ownership of some of the means of production, governmental distribution of some essential goods and services, and free elections.

13. _____ _____ is the percentage of unemployed persons in the labour force actively seeking jobs.

14. A _____ _____ combines the elements of a market economy (capitalism) with the elements of a command economy (socialism).

15. _____ _____ differ from the employment norms of the society in which they are located.

16. _____ _____ is part-time work or temporary work.

17. A _____ _____ is a group of employees who join together to bargain with an employer or a group of employers over wages, benefits, and working conditions.

Key People

Henry Ford *(p. 415)*

Milton Friedman *(p. 424)*

Harold Innis *(p. 402)*

Kari Levitt *(p. 403)*

Karl Marx *(p. 405)*

George Ritzer *(p. 415)*

Adam Smith *(p. 404)*

Frederick Winslow Taylor *(p. 414)*

Robert Wuthnow *(p. 408)*

Key People Quiz

Review of Key People – Matching Quiz

1. _____ Showed how the early Canadian economy was driven by the demands for raw materials by the colonial powers of France and Britain.

2. _____ Revolutionized management with a system he called *scientific management*.

3. _____ The founder of the Ford Motor Company, who incorporated hierarchical authority structures and scientific management techniques into the manufacturing process.

4. _____ Noted how the assembly line and machine technology have come to dominate work settings such as fast-food restaurants.

5. _____ Found that when people were asked about their most important reason for working, the most common response was "the money."

6. _____ Wrote *The Communist Manifesto* and *Das Kapital*, in which he predicted that the working class would become increasingly impoverished and alienated under capitalism.

7. _____ Was among the first to show how foreign private investment posed a threat to Canadian sovereignty as fundamental economic decisions were made outside the country.

8. _____ Advocated a policy of laissez-faire in his 1776 treatise, *An Inquiry into the Nature and Causes of the Wealth of Nations*.

9. _____ The winner of the Nobel prize for economics, who claimed that the only responsibility of business is to engage in activities designed to increase its profits.

a. Henry Ford
b. Milton Friedman
c. Harold Innis
d. Kari Levitt
e. Karl Marx
f. George Ritzer
g. Adam Smith
h. Frederick Winslow Taylor
i. Robert Wuthnow

Learning Objectives

After reading Chapter 13, the student should be able to:

1. describe the purpose of economy and distinguish between goods, services, labour, and capital (pp. 396–97).

2. describe what is meant by the sociology of economic life and explain how this differs from the study of economics (p. 397).

3. trace the major historical changes that have occurred in economic systems and note the most prevalent form of production found in each (pp. 397–402).

4. describe the four distinctive features of "ideal" capitalism and explain why pure capitalism does not exist (pp. 402–05).

5. define and distinguish between corporations and multinational corporations (pp. 402–03).

6. discuss socialism and describe its major characteristics (pp. 405–06).

7. compare and contrast capitalism, socialism, and mixed economies (pp. 402–07).

8. explain how the functionalist perspective views the economy and work (p. 407).

9. explain how the conflict perspective views the economy and work (pp. 407–08).

10. describe alienation and job satisfaction and explain the impact of each on workers (pp. 408–10).

11. note the relationship between gender and work as described by feminists (pp. 410–11).

12. discuss the major characteristics of professions (pp. 412–14).

13. compare scientific management (Taylorism) with mass production through automation (Fordism), noting the strengths and weaknesses of each (pp. 414–15).

14. identify the occupational categories considered to be marginal jobs and explain why they are classified as marginal (pp. 415–16).

15. define contingent work and explain how it benefits employers (pp. 416–17).

16. list and distinguish between the various types of unemployment (p. 418).

17. explain why the unemployment rate may not be a true reflection of unemployment in Canada (p. 418).

18. trace the development of labour unions and describe some of the means by which workers resist working conditions they consider to be oppressive (pp. 418–20).

19. explain why economist and futurist Jeremy Rifkin (1995) thinks that work as we know it is coming to an end (pp. 420–22).

20. note the major trends anticipated for the Canadian economy in the future and note the impact of globalization on these trends (pp. 422–25).

Unit Mastery Quizzes

Unit Mastery – Multiple Choice

1. Which of the following statements about historical economic systems is TRUE?
   a. Preindustrial economies are based on tertiary sector production.
   b. Industrial economies are based on secondary sector production.
   c. Postindustrial economies are based on the extraction of raw materials and natural resources from the environment.
   d. Postindustrial economies are based on the processing of raw materials into finished goods.

2. In order to maximize profits, capitalists often:
   a. suppress the wages of workers.
   b. reduce production because workers cannot purchase products.
   c. close factories and lay off workers.
   d. all of the above.

3. From a conflict perspective, business cycles are the result of:
   a. effort on the part of small-business owners.
   b. capitalist greed.
   c. surplus capital as a result of consumer spending.
   d. low interest rates.

4. How does a sociological perspective on the economy differ from the study of economics?
   a. Sociologists focus on the complex workings of economic systems.
   b. Economists are likely to study people's satisfaction with their jobs.
   c. Sociologists focus on the law of scarcity.
   d. Sociologists focus on the interconnections among the economy, other social institutions, and the social organization of work.

5. All of the following are key characteristics of professions EXCEPT:
   a. autonomy.
   b. self-regulation.
   c. job segmentation.
   d. authority.

6. The unemployment rate is not a complete measure of unemployment because:
   a. the rate does not include those who have stopped looking for work.
   b. the rate does not count students.
   c. a and b.
   d. none of the above.

7. In an effort to improve work conditions and gain some measure of control over their own work-related activities, workers:
   a. joined conglomerates.
   b. created an oligopoly.
   c. formed labour unions.
   d. alienated management until demands were met.

8. Which of the following is an essential component of the economy?
   a. goods and services
   b. labour
   c. capital
   d. all of the above make up the economy

9. Job satisfaction refers to people's attitudes toward their work based on:
    a. their job responsibilities.
    b. the organizational structure in which they work.
    c. their individual needs and values.
    d. all of the above.

10. A job is considered marginal if it:
    a. provides adequate pay with sufficient hours to make a living.
    b. is not covered by government work regulations, such as minimum standards of pay.
    c. is permanent.
    d. includes positions in the lower tier of the service sector.

11. According to Jeremy Rifkin's analysis:
    a. bank machines will replace tellers.
    b. robots will replace factory workers.
    c. knowledge workers (e.g., engineers) will benefit the most.
    d. all of the above will take place in the near future.

12. All of the following are major forms of unemployment EXCEPT:
    a. cyclical.
    b. marginal.
    c. seasonal.
    d. structural.

13. Large-scale organizations that have the legal power to buy and sell property separate from their individual owners are called:
    a. corporations.
    b. mixed economies.
    c. conglomerates.
    d. interlocking corporate directorates.

14. Ideal capitalism contains all of the following characteristics EXCEPT:
    a. private ownership of the means of production.
    b. pursuit of personal profit.
    c. competition.
    d. government intervention.

15. Private ownership of the means of production characterizes which type of economic system?
    a. capitalism
    b. socialism
    c. fascism
    d. none of the above

16. Which perspective views the economy as a vital institution because it is the means by which needed goods and services are provided and distributed?
    a. functionalist
    b. conflict
    c. feminist
    d. interactionist

17. Ideal socialism is based on:
    a. private ownership of the means of production.
    b. pursuit of individual goals.
    c. centralized decision making.
    d. all of the above.

18. The differential piece-rate system is a central component of:
    a. mass production through automation (Fordism).
    b. scientific management (Taylorism).
    c. management in bureaucracies.
    d. contingent work.

19. Part-time work or temporary employment is referred to as:
    a. marginal work.
    b. contingent work.
    c. personal service work.
    d. cyclical work.

20. These workers consist primarily of factory and craftworkers who do manual labour.
    a. blue-collar
    b. pink-collar
    c. white-collar
    d. green-collar

Unit Mastery – True or False

1. Goods are tangible objects that are necessary or desired (p. 396).
   TRUE or FALSE

2. Workers' skills are usually upgraded when new technology is introduced in the workplace (pp. 397–98).
   TRUE or FALSE

3. Capitalism involves the pursuit of collective goals (p. 405).
   TRUE or FALSE

4. Studies have found that worker satisfaction is highest when employees have some degree of control over their work (p. 409).
   TRUE or FALSE

5. Occupations are high-status, knowledge-based positions (p. 411).
   TRUE or FALSE

6. Positions in the lower tier of the service sector are characterized by low wages, little job security, and few chances for advancement (p. 415).

   TRUE or FALSE

7. Temporary workers make up the fastest-growing segment of the contingent work force (p. 417).

   TRUE or FALSE

8. Cyclical unemployment occurs because the skills demanded by employers do not match the skills of the unemployed (p. 418).

   TRUE or FALSE

9. Canada's regions have similar rates of unemployment (p. 418).

   TRUE or FALSE

10. Aboriginal Canadians have rates of unemployment that are more than double the national average (p. 418).

   TRUE or FALSE

Unit Mastery – Fill In the Blanks

1. _____ are intangible activities for which people are willing to pay (e.g., dry cleaning) (p. 396).

2. _____ consists of the physical and intellectual services, including training, education, and individual abilities, that people contribute to the production process (pp. 396–97).

3. _____ is the wealth (money or property) owned or used in business by a person or corporation (p. 397).

4. In _____ _____ , production is related primarily to producing food (p. 398).

5. A _____ _____ is based on the provision of services rather than goods (p. 400).

6. According to Heilbroner, _____ is not simply the accumulation of wealth, but the use of wealth to acquire more wealth (p. 402).

7. The early Canadian economy was based on the sale of _____ (goods associated with primary industries including lumber, wheat, and minerals) (p. 402).

8. In theory, _____ acts as a balance to excessive profits (p. 404).

9. Sweden and France have mixed economies, sometimes referred to as _____ _____ (p. 406).

10. _____ _____ refers to people's attitudes toward their work, based on their job responsibilities, the organizational structure in which they work, and their individual needs and values (p. 409).

Unit Mastery – Matching Quiz 1

Match the economy to its key characteristic:

1. _____ provision of services
2. _____ secondary sector production
3. _____ primary sector production

a. preindustrial economy
b. industrial economy
c. postindustrial economy

Unit Mastery – Matching Quiz 2

Match the economic system with its corresponding feature:

1. _____ public ownership of the means of production
2. _____ private and government ownership
3. _____ private ownership of the means of production

a. capitalism
b. socialism
c. mixed economy

Solutions

Key Terms Quiz

Review of Key Terms – Fill In the Blanks

1. Primary sector production
2. Secondary sector production
3. Postindustrial economy
4. Oligopoly
5. economy
6. Multinational corporations
7. Professions
8. Occupations
9. Socialism
10. Capitalism
11. Corporations
12. Democratic socialism
13. Unemployment rate
14. mixed economy
15. Marginal jobs
16. Contingent work
17. labour union

Key People Quiz

Review of Key People – Matching Quiz

1. C
2. H
3. A
4. F
5. I
6. E
7. D
8. G
9. B

Unit Mastery Quizzes

Unit Mastery – Multiple Choice

1. B
2. D
3. B
4. D
5. C
6. C
7. C
8. D
9. D
10. B
11. D
12. B
13. A
14. D
15. A
16. A
17. C
18. B
19. B
20. A

Unit Mastery – True or False

1. T
2. F, Jobs are often deskilled when new technology is installed in the workplace.
3. F, Socialism is an economic system characterized by public ownership of the means of production, the pursuit of collective goals, and centralized decision making.
4. T
5. F, Occupations are categories of jobs that involve similar activities at different work sites.
6. T
7. T
8. F, Cyclical unemployment occurs as a result of lower rates of production during recessions in the business cycle.
9. F, Canada's regions have widely different rates of unemployment.
10. T

Unit Mastery – Fill In the Blanks

1. Services
2. Labour
3. Capital
4. agrarian societies
5. postindustrial economy
6. capitalism
7. staples
8. competition
9. democratic socialism
10. Job satisfaction

Unit Mastery – Matching Quiz 1

1. C
2. B
3. A

Unit Mastery – Matching Quiz 2

1. B
2. C
3. A

Power, Politics, and Government

Chapter Outline

Chapter Summary

The relationship between politics and power is a strong one in all countries. Politics is the social institution through which power is acquired and exercised by some people or groups. Power is the ability of persons or groups to carry out their will even in the face of opposition. Most leaders, however, seek to legitimate their power. According to Max Weber, there are three types of authority: (1) charismatic, (2) traditional, and (3) rational-legal (bureaucratic). There are four main types of contemporary political systems: monarchy, authoritarianism, totalitarianism, and democracy. In a democracy the people hold the ruling power either directly or through elected representatives. According to the pluralist model, power in democratic governments is widely dispersed throughout many competing interest groups. In the elite model, power is concentrated among the elite, and the masses are relatively powerless. The power elite is composed of influential business leaders, key government leaders, and the military.

Political parties are organizations whose purpose is to gain and hold legitimate control of government. The Liberals and the Progressive Conservatives have dominated the Canadian political system since Confederation. People learn political attitudes, values, and behaviours through political socialization. Two challenging political issues in Canada are Quebec separatism and Aboriginal self-government. Transnational trends have made it increasingly difficult for all forms of governments to control events. While these trends will become more complex in the future, people are still likely to depend on their governments to lead and to provide solutions.

Key Terms

authoritarian political system *(p. 436)*

authority *(p. 432)*

charismatic authority *(p. 432)*

democracy *(p. 436)*

elite model *(p. 439)*

government *(p. 431)*

monarchy *(p. 436)*

pluralist model *(p. 438)*

political party *(p. 447)*

political socialization *(p. 448)*

politics *(p. 431)*

power *(p. 431)*

power elite *(p. 441)*

rational-legal authority *(p. 435)*

routinization of charisma *(p. 433)*

special interest groups *(p. 438)*

state *(p. 431)*

totalitarian political system *(p. 436)*

traditional authority *(p. 433)*

Key Terms Quiz

Review of Key Terms – Fill In the Blanks

1. _____ is the social institution through which power is acquired and exercised by some people and groups.

2. _____ is the political entity that possesses a legitimate monopoly over the use of force within its territory to achieve its goals.

3. _____ _____ is power that is legitimized by respect for long-standing custom.

4. _____ is the formal organization that has the legal and political authority to regulate the relationships among members of a society and between the society and those outside its borders.

5. _____ - _____ _____ is power legitimized by law or written rules and regulations.

6. _____ is a political system in which power resides in one person or family and is passed from generation to generation through lines of inheritance.

7. _____ _____ is composed of leaders at the top of business, the executive branch of the federal government, and the military.

8. _____ _____ is an organization whose purpose is to gain and hold legitimate control of government.

9. _____ is the ability of persons or groups to carry out their will despite opposition from others.

10. _____ _____ _____ occurs when charismatic authority is succeeded by a bureaucracy controlled by a rationally established authority or by a combination of traditional and bureaucratic authority.

11. _____ is power that people accept as legitimate rather than coercive.

12. In a _____ _____ power is widely dispersed throughout many competing interest groups.

13. _____ _____ is power legitimized on the basis of a leader's exceptional personal qualities.

14. _____ _____ _____ are political coalitions made up of individuals or groups that share a specific interest they wish to protect or advance with the help of the political system.

15. _____ _____ is a political system controlled by rulers who deny popular participation in government.

16. A _____ _____ is a political system in which the state seeks to regulate all aspects of people's public and private lives.

17. _____ is a political system in which the people hold the ruling power directly or through elected representatives.

18. According to the _____ _____ power in political systems is concentrated in the hands of a small group of elites, and the masses are relatively powerless.

19. _____ _____ is the process by which people learn political attitudes, values, and behaviour.

Key People

Ramsay Cook *(p. 456)*

Olive Dickason *(p. 452)*

G. William Domhoff *(p. 442)*

Emile Durkheim *(p. 438)*

Rand Dyck *(p. 439)*

Mary McIntosh *(p. 443)*

C. Wright Mills *(p. 441)*

Rick Ogmundson *(p. 449)*

Pierre Vallières *(p. 429)*

Max Weber *(p. 431)*

Key People Quiz

Review of Key People − Matching Quiz

1. _____ Pointed out that when the Europeans first came to North America, 55 Aboriginal First Nations were on the continent.

2. _____ Used the term "ruling class" to signify a relatively fixed group of privileged people who wield sufficient power to constrain political processes and serve underlying capitalist interests.

3. _____ Was among the first to formulate and test ideas concerning power elites.

4. _____ Was among the first to argue that gender issues were important considerations to politics and government.

5. _____ Predicted that pluralism will become even more important in the future.

6. _____ Claimed that the purpose of government is to socialize people to become good citizens, to regulate the economy so that it operates effectively, and to provide the necessary services for citizens.

7. _____ Examined the role of nationalism in justifying one's place in the world.

8. _____ Explained the weak link between class and voting in Canada.

9. _____ Claimed that force is not the most effective long-term means of gaining compliance because those who are being ruled do not accept as legitimate those who are doing the ruling.

10. _____ Was one of the intellectual leaders of the FLQ (the Front de Libération du Québec).

a. Ramsay Cook
b. Olive Dickason
c. G. William Domhoff
d. Emile Durkheim
e. Rand Dyck
f. Mary McIntosh
g. C. Wright Mills
h. Rick Ogmundson
i. Pierre Vallières
j. Max Weber

Learning Objectives

After reading Chapter 14, the student should be able to:

1. explain the relationship between politics, government, and the state (p. 431).

2. distinguish between power and authority (pp. 431−32).

3. define and describe what is meant by charismatic authority (pp. 432–33).

4. define and describe what is meant by traditional authority (pp. 433–35).

5. define and describe what is meant by rational-legal authority (p. 435).

6. describe the key features of monarchies (p. 436).

7. describe the key features of authoritarian systems (p. 436).

8. describe the key features of totalitarian systems (p. 436).

9. describe the key features of democracies (pp. 436–38).

10. state the major elements of pluralist (functionalist) models (p. 438).

11. define what special interests group are as well as what they hope to accomplish (p. 439).

12. state the major assumptions of elite (conflict) models and note the major contributions of C. Wright Mills and G. William Domhoff (pp. 439–42).

13. discuss how feminist perspectives view the political process (pp. 443–44).

14. summarize Gusfield's notion of a symbolic crusade (pp. 444–45).

15. discuss postmodern views on state influence on citizens (pp. 445–46).

16. define political party and describe the purpose of political parties (p. 447).

17. analyze how well Canadian parties measure up to the ideal-type characteristics of political parties (pp. 447–48).

18. explain the relationship between political socialization, political attitudes, and political participation (pp. 448–51).

19. discuss some of the causes and consequences of the Quiet Revolution and Quebec nationalism (pp. 451–52).

20. describe the case made by the Aboriginal peoples for self-government (pp. 452–55).

Unit Mastery Quizzes

Unit Mastery – Multiple Choice

1. According to Weber, _____ is power that is legitimized through formal rules and laws.
   a. rational-legal authority
   b. charismatic authority
   c. traditional authority
   d. exceptional authority

2. All of the following are true of monarchies EXCEPT:
   a. Power usually resides in one person or family.
   b. Power is passed on from generation to generation.
   c. Power is usually associated with rational-legal authority.
   d. Monarchies are most common in agrarian societies.

3. According to contemporary functionalists, the purpose of government is to:
   a. maintain law and order.
   b. plan and direct society.
   c. meet social needs.
   d. all of the above.

4. Which of the following statements best illustrates the relationship between politics and government?
   a. Politics involves government, but government does not involve politics.
   b. Politics is the ability of people to carry out their will, while government carries out orders regardless of people's will.
   c. In contemporary societies, the government is the primary political system.
   d. All of the above illustrate the relationship between politics and government.

5. Special interest groups:
   a. help people advocate their own interests and further their causes.
   b. can include broad categories such as banking, business, education, or labour.
   c. are sometimes referred to as pressure groups or lobbies.
   d. all of the above statements apply to special interest groups.

6. A group that is composed of people who develop policy positions, educate voters, and recruit candidates who agree with their policies is a:
   a. political party.
   b. political agenda.
   c. governmental bureaucracy.
   d. special interest group.

7. Traditional authority involves:
   a. charismatic leadership.
   b. respect for custom.
   c. legitimation through laws.
   d. all of the above.

8. Which of the following statements describes how Canadian political parties measure up to the ideal-type characteristics presented in the text?
   a. The two major parties rarely offer voters clear policy alternatives.
   b. Most political parties are dominated by active elites who are not representative of the general population.
   c. The electoral system in Canada effectively limits the degree to which a diversity of views will be reflected in our legislatures.
   d. All of the above are problems with Canadian political parties.

9. _____ is a political system in which dictators are likely to gain and hold the power.
   a. Monarchy
   b. Totalitarianism
   c. Democracy
   d. Authoritarianism

10. Totalitarianism is a political system in which:
    a.   the state seeks to regulate all aspects of people's lives.
    b.   rulers deny popular participation in government.
    c.   the people hold the ruling power.
    d.   citizens elect representatives to serve as bridges between themselves and the government.

11. Political participation includes:
    a.   voting.
    b.   attending and taking part in political meetings.
    c.   running for or holding political office.
    d.   all of the above demonstrate political participation.

12. According to Weber, charismatic authority is characterized by:
    a.   respect for long-standing custom.
    b.   legitimation through laws, rules, and regulations.
    c.   a leader's exceptional personal qualities.
    d.   none of the above.

13. According to Weber, patriarchy is most likely to characterize _____ type of authority.
    a.   charismatic
    b.   rational-legal
    c.   traditional
    d.   parliamentary

14. The literal meaning of democracy is:
    a.   thinking and behaving for oneself.
    b.   rule by the people.
    c.   absolute monarchy.
    d.   military dictatorship.

15. The key factor promoting Quebec separatism is:
    a.   hatred toward English Canadians.
    b.   a desire for unilingualism.
    c.   extreme Quebec nationalism.
    d.   a feeling of alienation.

16. _____ used the term "ruling class" to signify a relatively fixed group of privileged people who wield sufficient power to constrain political processes and serve underlying capitalist interests.
    a.   Menno Boldt
    b.   Thomas R. Dye
    c.   C. Wright Mills
    d.   G. William Domhoff

17. Which of the following statements about power and authority is TRUE?
    a. Power is when people accept things as legitimate because of charisma.
    b. People have a greater tendency to accept authority as legitimate if they are economically or politically dependent upon those who hold power.
    c. The most basic form of authority is force or military action.
    d. Power and authority cannot exist at the same time.

18. All of the following are major elements of elite (conflict) models of power EXCEPT:
    a. The masses have little influence over the elite and public policy.
    b. Individual rights are protected.
    c. Power is highly concentrated at the top of a pyramid-shaped social hierarchy; those at the top come together to set policy for everyone.
    d. Consensus exists among the elite as to the basic goals and values of society.

19. Which type of political model uses the government to impose the will of the powerful on the masses?
    a. elite model
    b. pluralist model
    c. functionalist model
    d. none of the above

20. Which statement concerning Aboriginal people in Canada is FALSE?
    a. Fifty-five Aboriginal First Nations were on the continent when Europeans first came to North America.
    b. Following Confederation, Aboriginal people came under the control of the government.
    c. Native people maintained full voting rights in federal elections from 1876 to present.
    d. As a consequence of the Indian Act, Aboriginal children were forced to attend residential schools.

Unit Mastery − True or False

1. Weber predicted that traditional authority would inhibit the development of capitalism (p. 434).
   TRUE or FALSE

2. Functionalist perspectives assume that government exists for the benefit of wealthy or politically powerful elites who use the government to impose their will on the masses (p. 441).
   TRUE or FALSE

3. The Elections Act of 1903 gave women the right to vote (p. 443).
   TRUE or FALSE

4. In Canada the party that wins the most seats in an election forms the government (p. 447).
   TRUE or FALSE

5. People's socioeconomic status affects their political attitudes and behaviours (p. 448).
   TRUE or FALSE

6. There is a very high association between social class and voting behaviour (p. 449).
   TRUE or FALSE

7. In Canada, about 25 percent of those eligible to vote exercise that right in federal elections (p. 450).
   TRUE or FALSE

8. Democracy has been defined as a government "of the people, by the people, and for the people" (p. 449).
   TRUE or FALSE

9. The Official Languages Act of 1969 made the federal public service bilingual (p. 452).
   TRUE or FALSE

10. Aboriginal people feel their status as Canada's first people entitles them to the right of self-determination and to protection of their culture and customs (p. 455).
    TRUE or FALSE

Unit Mastery – Fill In the Blanks

1. In contemporary society, the _____ is the primary political system (p. 431).

2. _____ is a social relationship that involves both leaders and followers (p. 431).

3. _____ refers to the process by which power is institutionalized and given a moral foundation to justify its existence (p. 432).

4. To Weber, _____ individuals are able to identify with the central facts or problems of people's lives and communicate their inspirations to others (p. 432).

5. With _____ - _____ _____ , the authority is invested in the office, not in the person who holds the office (p. 435).

6. A _____ - _____ is a unit of political organization that has recognizable national boundaries and whose citizens possess specific legal rights and obligations (p. 435).

7. In most democratic countries, including Canada, people have a voice in the government through _____ _____ , whereby citizens elect representatives to serve as bridges between themselves and the government (p. 437).

8. Both Canada and the United States are _____ , with a division of power between the central government and provincial or state governments (p. 437).

9. Postmodernists use the term _____ or _____ to describe the manner in which the state controls people in a less repressive fashion by providing them with incentives and by enlisting members of the community to encourage conforming behaviour (p. 445).

10. _____ tend to believe in limiting individual rights on social issues and to oppose social programs that they see as promoting individuals on the basis of minority status rather than merit (p. 448).

Unit Mastery – Matching Quiz 1

Match the political system with its main characteristic:

1. _____ state regulation
2. _____ ruled by the people
3. _____ power in one family
4. _____ denies popular participation

a. monarchy
b. authoritarianism
c. totalitarianism
d. democracy

Unit Mastery – Matching Quiz 2

Match the type of authority with its key feature:

1. _____ exceptional personal qualities
2. _____ written rules and regulations
3. _____ respect for custom

a. charismatic authority
b. traditional authority
c. rational-legal authority

Solutions

Key Terms Quiz

Review of Key Terms – Fill In the Blanks

1. Politics
2. State
3. Traditional authority
4. Government
5. Rational; legal authority
6. Monarchy
7. Power elite
8. Political party
9. Power
10. Routinization of charisma
11. Authority
12. pluralist model
13. Charismatic authority
14. Special interest groups
15. Authoritarian system
16. totalitarian system
17. Democracy
18. elite model
19. Political socialization

Key People Quiz

Review of Key People – Matching Quiz

1. B
2. C
3. G
4. F
5. E
6. D
7. A
8. H
9. J
10. I

Unit Mastery Quizzes

Unit Mastery – Multiple Choice

1. A
2. C
3. D
4. C
5. D
6. A
7. B
8. D
9. D
10. A
11. D
12. C
13. C
14. B
15. C
16. D
17. B
18. B
19. A
20. C

Unit Mastery – True or False

1. T
2. F, Conflict perspectives such as the elite model assume that the government exists for the benefit of the wealthy or powerful elites.
3. F, The Elections Act of 1903 forbade women from voting. They were not permitted to vote in federal elections until 1918.
4. T
5. T
6. F, Social class is correlated with political attitudes whereby the upper classes tend to be more conservative on economic issues while the lower class tends to be more conservative on social issues. However, there is less of a connection between voting behaviour and social class in Canada relative to other industrialized nations.
7. F, In Canada, the participation rate is currently about 61 percent (down from 75 percent in 1988).
8. T
9. T
10. T

Unit Mastery – Fill In the Blanks

1. government
2. Power
3. Legitimation
4. charismatic
5. rational; legal authority
6. nation; state
7. representative democracy
8. federations
9. governmentality; governance
10. Conservatives

Unit Mastery – Matching Quiz 1

1. C
2. D
3. A
4. B

Unit Mastery – Matching Quiz 2

1. A
2. C
3. B

Families and Intimate Relationships

Chapter Outline

Chapter Summary

Families (including those of gay men and lesbians) are relationships in which people live together with commitment, form an economic unit, care for any young, and consider their identity to be significantly attached to the group. Sociologists investigate marriage patterns (i.e., monogamy and polygamy), descent and inheritance patterns (i.e., patrilineal, matrilineal, and bilateral descent), as well as familial power and authority (i.e., patriarchal, matriarchal, and egalitarian families). Functionalists emphasize that families fulfill important societal functions, including sexual regulation, socialization of children, economic and psychological support, and the provision of social status. By contrast, conflict and feminist perspectives view the family as a source of social inequality and focus primarily on the problems inherent in relationships of dominance and subordination. Interactionists focus on family communication patterns and subjective meanings that members assign to everyday events. Postmodern perspectives try to provide insights into how family life has changed in the information age.

    Although cohabitation has become increasingly popular, some studies suggest that couples who cohabit report poorer-quality relationships than married couples. Communication and emotional support are crucial to the success of marriages. The difficulty in balancing work and family is a defining feature of life today. Women and men perform different household tasks, with women completing recurrent tasks that have specific times for completion (e.g., cooking, bathing a child) and men doing periodic tasks (e.g., mowing the lawn). One third of married couples choose to remain childless and, as a result of better contraception and assisted reproduction methods, fewer infants are available for adoption. Family violence and divorce are symptoms of dysfunctional relationships. Divorce has contributed to a dramatic increase in single-parent families and greater diversity in family relationships such as the creation of stepfamilies. The destruction of traditional Native families is evident in very high rates of parental abuse and neglect, suicide, physical, and sexual abuse. One of the main challenges of the next century will be to find effective strategies to reduce family violence and dysfunction.

Key Terms

bilateral descent *(p. 467)*

cohabitation *(p. 477)*

dual-earner families *(p. 479)*

egalitarian family *(p. 468)*

extended family *(p. 465)*

families *(p. 463)*

families we choose *(p. 463)*

family of orientation *(p. 464)*

family of procreation *(p. 465)*

heterosexism *(p. 488)*

homogamy *(p. 478)*

homophobia *(p. 483)*

infertility *(p. 480)*

kinship *(p. 464)*

marriage *(p. 465)*

matriarchal family *(p. 467)*

matrilineal descent *(p. 467)*

monogamy *(p. 465)*

nuclear family *(p. 465)*

patriarchal family *(p. 467)*

patriarchy *(p. 471)*

patrilineal descent *(p. 467)*

polyandry *(p. 466)*

polygamy *(p. 465)*

polygyny *(p. 465)*

second shift *(p. 479)*

sociology of family *(p. 469)*

Key Terms Quiz

Review of Key Terms – Fill In the Blanks

1. _____ refers to a situation where a couple lives together without being legally married.

2. _____ is marriage to one person at a time.

3. _____ _____ is a family composed of one or two parents and their dependent children, all of whom live apart from other relatives.

4. _____ _____ _____ are social arrangements that include intimate relationships between couples and close familial relationships with other couples and with other adults and children.

5. _____ _____ is a family structure in which authority is held by the eldest female.

6. _____ _____ is a family structure in which authority is held by the eldest male.

7. _____ _____ is a system of tracing descent through the mother's side of the family.

8. _____ _____ is a system of tracing descent through the father's side of the family.

9. _____ is a hierarchical system of social organization in which cultural, political, and economic structures are controlled by men.

10. _____ is an attitude in which heterosexuality is considered the only valid form of sexual behaviour, and gay men, lesbians, and bisexuals are seen as inferior to heterosexual people.

11. _____ is the concurrent marriage of a person of one sex with two or more members of the opposite sex.

12. _____ is the concurrent marriage of one woman with two or more men.

13. _____ is the concurrent marriage of one man with two or more women.

14. _____ _____ is the domestic work that employed women perform at home after they complete their workday on the job.

15. _____ are relationships in which people live together with commitment, form an economic unit and care for any young, and consider their identity to be significantly attached to the group.

16. _____ _____ is a system of tracing descent through both the mother's and father's sides of the family.

17. _____ - _____ _____ are families in which both partners are in the labour force.

18. _____ _____ is a family structure in which both partners share power and authority equally.

19. _____ _____ is a family unit composed of relatives in addition to parents and children who all live in the same household.

20. _____ _____ _____ is the subdiscipline of sociology that attempts to describe and explain patterns of family life and variations in family structure.

21. _____ is the pattern of individuals marrying those who have similar characteristics, such as race/ethnicity, religious background, age, education, or social class.

22. _____ refers to a hatred and fear of homosexuals and lesbians.

23. _____ is defined as an inability to conceive after one year of unprotected sexual relations.

24. _____ is a legally recognized and/or socially approved arrangement between two or more individuals that carries certain rights and obligations and usually involves sexual activity.

25. _____ is a social network of people based on common ancestry, marriage, or adoption.

26. _____ _____ _____ is the family into which a person is born and in which early socialization usually takes place.

27. _____ _____ _____ is the family that a person forms by having or adopting children.

Key People

Peter Berger and Hansfried Kellner *(p. 472)*

Jessie Bernard *(p. 472)*

Elizabeth Church *(p. 488)*

Emile Durkheim *(p. 469)*

David Elkind *(p. 472)*

Arlie Hochschild *(p. 479)*

Meg Luxton *(p. 471)*

Sara McLanahan and Karen Booth *(p. 482)*

Charlene Miall *(p. 481)*

Talcott Parsons *(p. 469)*

Key People Quiz

Review of Key People – Matching Quiz

1. _____ Argued from a functionalist view that marriage is a replica of the larger society.

2. _____ Claimed that interaction between marital partners contributes to a shared reality.

3. _____ Outlined the instrumental and expressive roles of husbands and wives.

4. _____ Argued that women and men experience marriage differently.

5. _____ Highlighted the dependency created in patriarchal family systems.

6. _____ Explained how involuntarily childless women engage in "information management" to combat social stigma.

7. _____ Suggests that, given the divorce rate in Canada, divorce should no longer be viewed as a deviant act, but rather a normal part of many people's lives.

8. _____ Claimed that children in mother-only families are more likely than children in two-parent families to have poor academic achievement, higher divorce rates, and more involvement in alcohol and drugs.

9. _____ Coined the term "second shift" to describe the domestic work that employed women perform at home.

10. _____ Describes the postmodern family as permeable.

a. Peter Berger and Hansfried Kellner

b. Jessie Bernard

c. Elizabeth Church

d. Emile Durkheim

e. Arlie Hochschild

f. Meg Luxton

g. Sara McLanahan and Karen Booth

h. Charlene Miall

i. David Elkind

j. Talcott Parsons

Learning Objectives

After reading Chapter 15, the student should be able to:

1. define families and families we choose and explain why it has become increasingly difficult to develop a concise definition of the family (pp. 463–64).

2. distinguish between family of orientation and procreation, and distinguish between extended and nuclear families (pp. 464–65).

3. define marriage and indicate what form is legally sanctioned in Canada (p. 465).

4. define polygamy and distinguish between its two forms (pp. 465–67).

5. discuss the system of descent and inheritance, and explain why such systems are important in societies (p. 467).

6. distinguish between patriarchal, matriarchal, and egalitarian families (pp. 467–69).

7. note the emphasis of a functionalist perspective on families and describe the four key functions of families in industrial societies (pp. 469–70).

8. describe how the conflict and feminist perspectives view families (pp. 470–72).

9. outline the key assumptions of symbolic interactionist perspectives on the family (p. 472).

10. describe some characteristics of the postmodern family (pp. 472–74).

11. note attitudes toward and involvement in the use of the Internet to find a mate (pp. 475–76).

12. define cohabitation and note changes in attitudes toward cohabitation over the past two decades (pp. 477–78).

13. note some of the reasons for getting married and indicate what kind of marriage partners Canadians tend to choose for themselves (pp. 478–79).

14. explain the concepts "dual-earner" and "second shift" (pp. 479–80).

15. distinguish between the terms "child-free" and "childless" and discuss whether couples need to have children to be happy (p. 480).

16. discuss the major issues associated with adoption, new reproductive technologies, and single-parent households (pp. 481–83).

17. note the major trends in remarriage (pp. 483–84).

18. note why sociologists have difficulty studying family violence and be familiar with the key findings from the 2005 General Social Survey on Victimization (pp. 484–86).

19. explain the major causes and consequences of divorce in Canada (pp. 486–88).

20. describe the diversity found in contemporary Canadian families (pp. 488–92).

Unit Mastery Quizzes

Unit Mastery – Multiple Choice

1. The marriage of one woman with two or more men at the same time is called:
   a. monogamy.
   b. polyandry.
   c. polygyny.
   d. serial monogamy.

2. These families often include grandparents, uncles, aunts, or other relatives who live in the same household.
   a. blended
   b. extended
   c. nuclear
   d. foster

3. Which of the following statements about cohabitation is FALSE?
   a. Cohabiting partners are often not as committed to their relationship as married couples are.
   b. Those most likely to cohabit are young adults between the ages of 25 and 29.
   c. The number of cohabiting couples is decreasing in Canada.
   d. The census defines common-law partners as two persons of the opposite sex who are not legally married but live together as husband and wife.

4. According to recent research on cyberdating:
   a. Romance was the primary goal of Internet use among students.
   b. Most respondents were unsuccessful in meeting someone online.
   c. Anxiety reduction was a major benefit of using the Internet to meet new people.
   d. Sex was the focus of cyberdating for most students.

5. _____ refers to a social network of people based on common ancestry, marriage, or adoption.
   a. Union
   b. Extended family
   c. Kinship
   d. Family tie

6. In what kind of family structure does the eldest female have authority?
   a. patriarchal
   b. matriarchal
   c. egalitarian
   d. bilateral

7. Which of the following is a major cause of divorce?
   a. Marriage at an early age.
   b. Limited economic resources and low wages.
   c. The presence of children.
   d. All of the above are major causes of divorce.

8. Which of the following statements best describes shifts in Canadian family structure from 1981 to 2001?
   a. The number of common-law couples (with and without children) has increased.
   b. The number of common-law couples with children has decreased.
   c. The number of lone-parent families has decreased.
   d. The number of married couples with children has increased.

9. In which pattern of descent is inheritance traced through the father's side of the family?
   a. patrilineal
   b. matrilineal
   c. bilateral
   d. unilateral

10. Interactionists explain family relationships in terms of:
    a. men's domination over women.
    b. sources of social inequality and exploitation.
    c. the subjective meanings and everyday interpretations people give to their lives.
    d. functions performed at a macrolevel.

11. All of the following are key functions of the family EXCEPT:
    a. sexual regulation.
    b. socialization.
    c. economic and psychological support.
    d. all of the above are key functions of the family.

12. Today's families do not fit the standard sociological definition due to the prevalence of:
    a. single-parent households.
    b. lesbian and gay couples.
    c. common-law couples.
    d. all of the above.

13. In this family structure, both partners share power and authority equally.
    a. patriarchal
    b. matriarchal
    c. egalitarian
    d. bilateral

14. _____ have been primarily responsible for redefining the concept of "the family," focusing on the diversity of family arrangements.
    a. Conflict theorists
    b. Feminist theorists
    c. Symbolic interactionists
    d. Functionalists

15. _____ view the communication process in families as integral to the roles that different family members play.
    a. Postmodern theorists
    b. Feminist theorists
    c. Symbolic interactionists
    d. Functionalists

16. _____ note that definitions concerning family violence are socially constructed and have an effect on how people are treated.
    a. Conflict theorists
    b. Feminist theorists
    c. Symbolic interactionists
    d. Postmodernists

17. _____ focus on class and property arrangements as the main source of inequality in the family.
    a. Conflict theorists
    b. Feminist theorists
    c. Symbolic interactionists
    d. Functionalists

18. _____ describe the family as being permeable or capable of being diffused in such a manner that its original purpose is changed.
    a. Postmodernists
    b. Feminist theorists
    c. Symbolic interactionists
    d. Conflict theorists

19. Which of the followings statements about remarriage is FALSE?
    a. Most people who get divorced remarry.
    b. Most divorced people remarry others who have been divorced.
    c. Women with a university degree and without children tend to remarry relatively quickly.
    d. At all ages, a greater proportion of men than women remarry.

20. Which of the following statements about families in Canada is FALSE?
    a. Nuclear families are smaller in size than they were twenty years ago.
    b. In Canada, the only legally sanctioned form of marriage is monogamy.
    c. In households where women are the primary breadwinners, the males do the majority of housework.
    d. Most people in Canada tend to choose marriage partners who are similar to themselves in terms of ethnicity, age, education, and social class.

Unit Mastery − True or False

1. Divorce is the legal process of dissolving a marriage that allows former spouses to remarry if they choose (p. 486).
    TRUE or FALSE

2. The presence of children helps marriages stay together (p. 487).
    TRUE or FALSE

3. One out of every two marriages ends in divorce (p. 464).
    TRUE or FALSE

4. Polygamy is against the law in Canada (pp. 465–66).
    TRUE or FALSE

5. Women who have not graduated from high school and have young children tend to remarry relatively quickly following divorce (p. 483).
    TRUE or FALSE

6. In Canada, adoption is regulated provincially (p. 481).
    TRUE or FALSE

7. In gestational surrogacy, the sperm and eggs from the infertile couple are transferred to the surrogate using an assisted reproductive technology (p. 482).
    TRUE or FALSE

8. The vast majority of single-parent families are headed by females (p. 482).
    TRUE or FALSE

9. In Canada, gay and lesbian couples have been able to legally marry for more than a decade (p. 488).
    TRUE or FALSE

10. The destruction of the traditional Aboriginal family was the result of interventionist strategies employed by the Canadian church and state (p. 492).
    TRUE or FALSE

Unit Mastery – Fill In the Blanks

1. Through a pattern of marriage, divorce, and remarriage, some people practise _____ _____ , a succession of marriages in which a person has several spouses over a lifetime (p. 465).

2. _____ often involves the marriage of a woman to two or more brothers (p. 466).

3. A traditional definition specifies that a _____ family is made up of a "couple" and their dependent children (p. 465).

4. In Canada, the only legally sanctioned form of marriage is _____ (p. 465).

5. The most prevalent form of polygamy is _____ , the marriage of one man to more than one woman (p. 465).

6. The _____ of _____ is the subdiscipline of sociology that attempts to describe and explain patterns of family life (p. 469).

7. _____ perspectives on the family focus on patriarchy rather than class as a major source of inequality (p. 471).

8. The work carried out by women at home following their workday on the job is known as the _____ _____ (p. 479).

9. _____ families consist of a husband, wife, children from previous marriages, and children (if any) from the new marriage (pp. 483–84).

10. To the Ojibwa, _____ referred to individuals who worked together and were bound together by responsibility and friendships as well as kinship ties (p. 492).

Unit Mastery – Matching Quiz 1

Match the marriage pattern to its defining feature:

1. _____ one partner at a time   a. monogamy
2. _____ one wife, two husbands   b. polygyny
3. _____ one husband, two wives   c. polyandry

Unit Mastery – Matching Quiz 2

Match the pattern of descent to its key characteristic:

1. _____ a legitimate son inherits his father's property   a. patrilineal descent
2. _____ property and position is traced from the maternal uncle to his nephew   b. matrilineal descent   c. bilateral descent
3. _____ kinship is traced through both parents

Unit Mastery – Matching Quiz 3

Match the theorist group to its core focus:

1. _____ focus on the role of families in maintaining stability of society   a. functionalists
2. _____ focus on families as patriarchal institutions   b. conflict theorists   c. feminists
3. _____ focus on families as sources of social inequality   d. symbolic interactionists
4. _____ focus on the permeability of families   e. postmodernists
5. _____ focus on family dynamics including communication patterns

Solutions

Key Terms Quiz

Review of Key Terms − Fill In the Blanks

1. Cohabitation
2. Monogamy
3. Nuclear family
4. Families we choose
5. Matriarchal family
6. Patriarchal family
7. Matrilineal descent
8. Patrilineal descent
9. Patriarchy
10. Heterosexism
11. Polygamy
12. Polyandry
13. Polygyny
14. Second shift
15. Families
16. Bilateral descent
17. Dual; earner families
18. Egalitarian family
19. Extended family
20. Sociology of family
21. Homogamy
22. Homophobia
23. Infertility
24. Marriage
25. Kinship
26. Family of orientation
27. Family of procreation

Key People Quiz

Review of Key People − Matching Quiz

1. D
2. A
3. J
4. B
5. F
6. H
7. C
8. G
9. E
10. I

Unit Mastery Quizzes

Unit Mastery − Multiple Choice

1. B
2. B
3. C
4. C
5. C
6. B
7. D
8. A
9. A
10. C
11. D
12. D
13. C
14. B
15. C
16. C
17. A
18. A
19. C
20. C

Unit Mastery − True or False

1. T
2. F, The presence of children (depending on their gender and age at the beginning of the marriage) is a risk factor for divorce.
3. F, Canadian estimates based on a cohort approach are that 35 to 40 percent of marriages will end in divorce.
4. T
5. T
6. T
7. T
8. T
9. F, As of July 2005, same-sex couples are able to legally marry, but this is still a hotly debated and divisive issue for the Canadian public.
10. T

Unit Mastery − Fill In the Blanks

1. serial monogamy
2. Polyandry
3. nuclear
4. monogamy
5. polygyny
6. sociology; family
7. Feminist
8. second shift
9. Blended
10. family

Unit Mastery − Matching Quiz 1

1. A
2. C
3. B

Unit Mastery − Matching Quiz 2

1. A
2. B
3. C

Unit Mastery − Matching Quiz 3

1. A
2. C
3. B

4. E   5. D

CHAPTER **16**

Education

Chapter Outline

Chapter Summary

Education is the social institution responsible for the systematic transmission of knowledge, skills, and cultural values within a formally organized structure. People in preliterate societies acquire knowledge and skills through informal education, while education is more formalized in preindustrial and industrial societies. Functionalists focus on how education contributes to socialization, transmission of culture, social control, social placement, and innovation, while conflict theorists emphasize how education perpetuates class, racial-ethnic, and gender inequalities. Feminists note how gender bias is prevalent in both the hidden and formal curriculum. Symbolic interactionists point out that education may be a self-fulfilling prophecy for students who perform in accordance with teacher expectations. Postmodernists point out the wide diversity of family systems recognized in the school system and note how higher education is being shaped by a "students as consumers" model.

Although education costs more and is perceived to be of a higher quality in private schools versus public ones, there is little research to support this belief. The overall rate of school dropout has significantly decreased in recent decades, with those who drop out citing reasons that include a dislike of school, a belief that school is a waste of time, and general skepticism regarding the value of education. There is growing dissatisfaction among parents and students about the quality of education, which is believed to have declined largely as a result of child-centred education programs. Although most women in Canada have greater educational opportunities than those living in developing nations, their educational opportunities are not equal to those of males in their social class. Another issue is how to provide better educational opportunities for students with disabilities. As governments cut their funding to higher education, the costs of postsecondary education are falling more to parents and students. Controversies that will continue to have an impact on education in the future include questions about what should be taught in schools, demand for greater accountability for student outcomes, alternatives to public schooling such as home-based schooling, and the use of information technologies.

Key Terms

credentialism *(p. 508)*

cultural capital *(p. 506)*

cultural transmission *(p. 499)*

education *(p. 499)*

formal education *(p. 500)*

functional illiteracy *(p. 516)*

hidden curriculum *(p. 508)*

informal education *(p. 500)*

mass education *(p. 501)*

tracking *(p. 507)*

Key Terms Quiz

Review of Key Terms – Fill In the Blanks

1. _____ is the social institution responsible for the systematic transmission of knowledge, skills, and cultural values within a formally organized structure.

2. _____ _____ is the transmission of cultural values and attitudes, such as conformity and obedience to authority, through implied demands found in rules, routines, and regulations of schools.

3. _____ is a process of social selection in which class advantage and social status are linked to the possession of academic qualifications.

4. _____ _____ is a term used for social assets that include values, beliefs, attitudes, and competencies in language and culture.

5. _____ is the assignment of students to specific courses and educational programs based on their test scores, previous grades, or both.

6. _____ _____ is the inability to read and/or write at the skill level necessary for carrying out everyday tasks.

7. _____ _____ is a term for learning that takes place within an academic setting such as school, which has a planned instructional process and teachers who convey specific knowledge, skills, and thinking processes to students.

8. _____ _____ is the process by which children and recent immigrants become acquainted with the dominant cultural beliefs, values, norms, and accumulated knowledge of society.

9. _____ _____ is a term for learning that occurs in a spontaneous, unplanned way.

10. _____ _____ is a term used for providing free, public schooling for wide segments of a nation's population.

Key People

Pierre Bourdieu *(p. 506)*

Emile Durkheim *(p. 504)*

Richard J. Herrnstein and Charles Murray *(p. 511)*

Wendy Luttrell *(p. 506)*

Jeannie Oakes *(p. 507)*

Key People Quiz

Review of Key People – Matching Quiz

1. _____ Studied working class women who returned to school after dropping out and noted that schools play a critical role in class reproduction and self-identity.
2. _____ Used a functionalist perspective to argue the fundamental importance of education in society.
3. _____ Coined the term "cultural capital."
4. _____ Argued that intelligence is genetically inherited and that people cannot be "smarter" than they were born.
5. _____ Found that tracking affects students' academic achievements and career choices.

a. Pierre Bourdieu
b. Emile Durkheim
c. Richard J. Herrnstein and Charles Murray
d. Wendy Luttrell
e. Jeannie Oakes

Learning Objectives

After reading Chapter 16, the student should be able to:

1. define education (p. 499).
2. note what informal education in preliterate societies consists of (pp. 499–500).
3. note the changes in formal education from preindustrial to industrial and postindustrial societies (pp. 500–02).
4. define mass education (p. 501).
5. describe education in Japan (pp. 502–03).
6. describe education in Bosnia (p. 503).
7. describe how a functionalist perspective views education and be able to list the five key manifest functions of education (pp. 504–05).
8. understand how latent functions differ from manifest ones and be able to identify the three key latent functions of education (pp. 505–06).
9. describe the conflict perspectives' view of education as a vehicle for class reproduction and be able to define cultural capital (p. 506).
10. define tracking and explain how this process is related to social inequality (pp. 506–07).
11. explain how the conflict perspective defines the "hidden curriculum" and note the implications of the hidden curriculum for social class and credentialism (p. 508).
12. note how gender bias is embedded in the formal and hidden curriculums of school (pp. 508–09).

13. discuss symbolic interactionist perspectives on education and describe the significance of the self-fulfilling prophecy and labelling on educational achievement (pp. 511–12).

14. explain why postmodern perspectives view education as characterized by permeability and explain what is meant by the term "McUniversity" (pp. 512–13).

15. note the differences (perceived and real) between public and private schools (p. 515).

16. be familiar with the trends in school dropout rates and list some of the common reasons why students drop out of school (pp. 515–16).

17. report evidence for a decline in academic standards and note some of the reasons given for this decline (pp. 516–18).

18. describe some of the steps taken to equalize opportunities for students with disabilities (pp. 518–19).

19. describe characteristics of people who obtain postsecondary educations and note the implications of funding for obtaining a postsecondary education (pp. 519–21).

20. describe the issues that will continue to be important considerations for the future of education in Canada (pp. 521–23).

Unit Mastery Quizzes

Unit Mastery – Multiple Choice

1. Which of the following statements about formal education in historical and global perspectives is FALSE?
   a. In all societies, people must acquire certain knowledge and skills in order to survive.
   b. As societies industrialize, the need for formal education of the masses increases significantly.
   c. Formal education originated in preliterate societies.
   d. The Renaissance and the Industrial Revolution had a profound impact on education.

2. Suppose a boy learns to hunt and fish by observing his father and grandfather. This type of learning is called:
   a. informal
   b. formal
   c. preliterate
   d. semiliterate

3. Which of the following statements about education in Canada is FALSE?
   a. Children of parents with high levels of education are more likely to pursue postsecondary education.
   b. Aboriginal peoples are underrepresented among postsecondary graduates relative to their presence in the overall population.
   c. Canada has the largest percentage of the population with postsecondary education of any developed nation.
   d. Women and men earn about the same number of degrees in Canada each year.

4. Which of the following is a latent function of education?
   a. restricting some activities
   b. matchmaking and production of social networks
   c. creation of a generation gap
   d. all of the above are latent functions of education

5. Which perspective is most likely to examine higher education from a "students-as-consumers" model?
   a. functionalist
   b. conflict
   c. postmodernist
   d. symbolic interactionist

6. Japanese schools emphasize:
   a. conformity and nationalism.
   b. the importance of obligation to one's family.
   c. the importance of learning the skills necessary for employment.
   d. all of the above.

7. Socialization, transmission of culture, and social control are:
   a. manifest functions of education.
   b. latent functions of education.
   c. mandatory functions of education.
   d. hidden functions of education.

8. Which perspective argues that schools perpetuate class, racial-ethnic, and gender inequalities in society?
   a. functionalist
   b. conflict
   c. interactionist
   d. postmodern

9. Much of the blame for declining academic standards in the 1980s and 1990s has been directed at:
   a. a lack of parents' interest in their children's school achievement.
   b. increased parental work hours and decreased parental time spent helping children with homework.
   c. an inability to find enough new teachers with higher academic qualifications.
   d. educational reforms focusing on child-centred education.

10. Home-based schooling has been criticized on the grounds that:
    a. the average parent may not be able to cover all areas of the curriculum.
    b. appropriate program materials may not be available.
    c. there is an absence of social interaction.
    d. all of the above are criticisms of home-based schooling.

11. Which of the following statements about current issues in education is FALSE?
    a. The overall school dropout rate is increasing.
    b. An increasing number of parents are dissatisfied with the quality of their children's education.
    c. The education system does not always provide a supportive atmosphere for girls and may undermine their confidence.
    d. The barriers facing students with disabilities are slowly being removed or surmounted by new legislation.

12. Which of the following factors contributes to the reproduction of class:
    a. Middle- and upper-class parents endow their children with high cultural capital, which results in higher chances of success in school.
    b. Many Canadian schools practise streaming or tracking of children in various courses and programs.
    c. Student records, test scores, dress, appearance, parental background, sex, and ethnicity combine in a very complex way to affect teacher expectations and evaluations.
    d. All of the above contribute to the reproduction of class.

13. Which perspective focuses on classroom communication patterns and educational practices that affect students' self-concept and aspirations?
    a. functionalist
    b. conflict
    c. interactionist
    d. feminist

14. Which perspective claims that the process of labelling is directly related to the power and status of those persons who do the labelling and those who are being labelled?
    a. functionalist
    b. conflict
    c. interactionist
    d. postmodern

15. Which perspective claims that students from all classes are subject to a hidden curriculum?
    a. functionalist
    b. conflict
    c. interactionist
    d. realist

16. Which perspective emphasizes the importance of shared values within an education system that are transmitted from kindergarten through university?
    a. functionalist
    b. conflict
    c. interactionist
    d. feminist

17. What percentage of students drop out before completing high school?
    a. approximately 2 percent
    b. approximately 12 percent
    c. approximately 22 percent
    d. approximately 32 percent

18. Which of the following statements about the "hidden curriculum" is FALSE?
    a. Students from all social classes are subjected to the hidden curriculum.
    b. Middle- and upper-class students may be most adversely affected by the hidden curriculum.
    c. The hidden curriculum in the early grades encourages students to be competitive, materialistic, to value work over play, and to show deference to authority.
    d. Students from lower-class backgrounds are less motivated when rewards for effort are symbolic rather than material.

19. Free, public schooling for wide segments of a nation's population is known as:
    a. subsidized education.
    b. public education.
    c. global education.
    d. mass education.

20. All of the following are manifest functions of formal education EXCEPT:
    a. socialization.
    b. transmission of culture.
    c. matchmaking and production of social networks.
    d. change and innovation.

Unit Mastery – True or False

1. Formal education has taken place throughout human history (pp. 499–500).
   TRUE or FALSE

2. By the early 1800s, mass education had taken hold in Canada, as the provinces established free, tax-supported elementary schools (p. 501).
   TRUE or FALSE

3. Functionalists suggest that education contributes to the maintenance of society and provides people with an opportunity for self-enhancement and upward social mobility (p. 504).
   TRUE or FALSE

4. An example of a manifest function of education is the creation of a generation gap (p. 506).
   TRUE or FALSE

5. Research indicates that ability grouping and tracking affects students' academic achievements and career choices (pp. 506–07).
   TRUE or FALSE

6. Middle- and upper-income parents endow their children with more cultural capital than do working-class and poverty-level parents (p. 506).

   TRUE or FALSE

7. Most parents are very satisfied with the quality of their children's education (p. 516).

   TRUE or FALSE

8. Many schools have attempted to mainstream children with disabilities through the use of inclusion programs (p. 518).

   TRUE or FALSE

9. According to symbolic interactionists, the process of labelling is directly related to power and status of those persons who do the labelling and those who are being labelled (p. 511).

   TRUE or FALSE

10. Recent trends suggest that access to education is becoming more restricted as a result of funding cuts at both the provincial and federal levels (p. 523).

    TRUE or FALSE

Unit Mastery – Fill In the Blanks

1. _____ _____ involves the "proper" attitudes toward education, socially approved dress and manners, and knowledge about books, art, music, and other forms of high and popular culture (p. 506).

2. Educational credentials are extremely important in societies that emphasize _____ , a process of social selection in which class advantage and social status are linked to the possession of academic qualifications (p. 508).

3. The _____ _____ has been used to explain why so few women study mathematics and science (p. 508).

4. _____ societies have no written language and are characterized by very basic technology and a simple division of labour (p. 499).

5. _____ _____ is learning that takes place within an academic setting such as a school, which has a planned instructional process and teachers who convey specific knowledge, skills, and thinking processes to students (p. 500).

6. Durkheim asserted that a _____ education is very important because it conveys values that are the foundation of a cohesive social order (p. 504).

7. The open, stated, and intended goals or consequences of activities within an organization or institution are known as _____ functions (p. 504).

8. _____ is the assignment of students to specific courses and educational programs based on their test scores, previous grades, or both (p. 507).

9. According to conflict theorists, _____ is not driven by an actual need for increased knowledge, but rather by the desire on the part of the members of professional groups to protect their own vested interests, namely income, prestige, autonomy, and power (p. 508).

10. In the 1980s and 1990s, educational reforms included the implementation of _____ - _____ education, a system of learning that encourages students to progress at their own rate (p. 516).

Unit Mastery − Matching Quiz 1

Match the concept with the appropriate theoretical perspective on education:

1.	_____ functionalist perspective	a.	manifest functions
2.	_____ conflict perspective	b.	difference and irregularity
3.	_____ symbolic interactionist perspective	c.	self-fulfilling prophecy
4.	_____ postmodern perspective	d.	cultural capital

Unit Mastery − Matching Quiz 2

Match the educational practice with the appropriate country:

1.	_____ Canada	a.	emphasis on obligation to one's family
2.	_____ Japan	b.	ethnically segregated history classes
3.	_____ Bosnia	c.	controversy over what should be taught

Solutions

Key Terms Quiz

Review of Key Terms – Fill In the Blanks

1. Education
2. Hidden curriculum
3. Credentialism
4. Cultural capital
5. Tracking
6. Functional illiteracy
7. Formal education
8. Cultural transmission
9. Informal education
10. Mass education

Key People Quiz

Review of Key People – Matching Quiz

1. E
2. B
3. A
4. D
5. C

Unit Mastery Quizzes

Unit Mastery – Multiple Choice

1. C
2. A
3. D
4. D
5. C
6. D
7. A
8. B
9. D
10. D
11. A
12. D
13. C
14. C
15. B
16. A
17. B
18. B
19. D
20. C

Unit Mastery – True or False

1. F, People in preindustrial societies gained knowledge through informal education. The earliest formal education occurred in ancient Greece and Rome.
2. F, Mass education took hold in Canada in the early 1900s, as provinces established free, tax-supported elementary schools.
3. T
4. F, The generation gap is a latent, or unintended consequence of education.
5. T
6. T
7. F, Across Canada, thousands of parents are expressing concerns that the public school system is doing a poor job of teaching their children.
8. T
9. T
10. T

Unit Mastery – Fill In the Blanks

1. Cultural capital
2. credentialism
3. hidden curriculum
4. Preliterate
5. Formal education
6. moral
7. manifest
8. Tracking
9. credentialism
10. child; centred

Unit Mastery – Matching Quiz 1

1. A
2. D
3. C
4. B

Unit Mastery – Matching Quiz 2

1. C
2. A
3. B

Religion

Chapter Outline

Chapter Summary

Religion is a system of beliefs, symbols, and rituals, based on some sacred realm that guides human behaviour, gives meaning to life, and unites believers into a community. Religions have been categorized as simple supernaturalism, animism, theism, and transcendent idealism, depending upon their dominant belief. According to functionalists, religion provides meaning to life, promotes social cohesion, and contributes to social control. From a conflict perspective, the capitalist class uses religion as a tool of domination to mislead workers about their true interests. Symbolic interactionists examine the meanings that people give to religion and religious symbols in their everyday life. Feminist perspectives point out that women and men experience the same religion differently. The gender-inclusiveness of Christianity and Judaism and the absence of women in significant roles within religious institutions is becoming increasingly important to women. Postmodernists attempt to explain the coexistence of secularization in some parts of the world and the spread of religion elsewhere. Contemporary religious organizations include ecclesia, churches, denominations, sects, and cults. Many Canadians have turned away from the church for various reasons, including a belief that church attendance is not the best way to express commitment, debates around homosexuality, marginalization of women, and child sexual abuse by ministers and priests.

Key Terms

animism *(p. 532)*

church *(p. 543)*

cult *(p. 544)*

denomination *(p. 543)*

ecclesia *(p. 543)*

faith *(p. 531)*

liberation theology *(p. 552)*

monotheism *(p. 532)*

nontheistic religion *(p. 532)*

polytheism *(p. 532)*

profane *(p. 531)*

religion *(p. 528)*

rituals *(p. 531)*

sacred *(p. 531)*

sect *(p. 543)*

simple supernaturalism *(p. 532)*

theism *(p. 532)*

Key Terms Quiz

Review of Key Terms – Fill In the Blanks

1. A _____ is a religious group with practices and teaching outside the dominant cultural and religious traditions of a society.

2. _____ is a system of beliefs, symbols, and rituals, based on some sacred or supernatural realm, that guides human behaviour, gives meaning to life, and unites believers into a community.

3. _____ is the belief that plants, animals, or other elements of the natural world are endowed with spirits or life forces that have an impact on events in society.

4. _____ are regularly repeated and carefully prescribed forms of behaviour that symbolize a cherished value or belief.

5. A _____ is a large, bureaucratically organized religious body that tends to seek accommodation with the larger society in order to maintain some degree of control over it.

6. _____ is unquestioning belief that does not require proof or scientific evidence.

7. _____ _____ is a religion based on a belief in divine spiritual forces such as sacred principles of thought and conduct, rather than a god or gods.

8. _____ is a belief in more than one god.

9. _____ is the everyday, secular, or "worldly" aspects of life.

10. _____ are those aspects of life that are extraordinary or supernatural.

11. _____ is a belief in a single, supreme being or god who is responsible for significant events such as the creation of the world.

12. _____ _____ is the belief that supernatural forces affect people's lives either positively or negatively.

13. A _____ is a relatively small religious group that has broken away from another religious organization to renew what it views as the original version of the faith.

14. _____ is a religious organization that is so integrated into the dominant culture that it claims as its membership all members of a society.

15. _____ _____ is the Christian movement that advocates freedom from political subjugation within a traditional perspective and the need for social transformation to benefit the poor and downtrodden.

16. _____ is a large, organized religious body characterized by accommodation to society but frequently lacking the ability or intention to dominate society.

17. _____ is a belief in god or gods.

Key People

Peter Berger *(p. 531)*

Emile Durkheim *(p. 533)*

Clifford Geertz *(p. 531)*

John Lofland and Rodney Stark *(p. 536)*

Karl Marx *(p. 534)*

Keith A. Roberts *(p. 530)*

Max Weber *(p. 534)*

Key People Quiz

Review of Key People – Matching Quiz 1

1. _____ Wanted to find out why people converted to nontraditional religious movements.
2. _____ Was one of the first sociologists to emphasize that religion is essential to the maintenance of society.
3. _____ Referred to religion as a sacred canopy that gives people security and answers to the questions of life.
4. _____ An anthropologist who claimed that religion is a set of cultural symbols that establish powerful and pervasive moods and motivations to help people interpret the meaning of life and establish direction for their behaviour.

a. Peter Berger
b. Emile Durkheim
c. Clifford Geertz
d. John Lofland and Rodney Stark

Review of Key People – Matching Quiz 2

1. _____ Believed that religion served as a catalyst for social change.
2. _____ Claimed that beliefs are only a small part of the sociological examination of religion.
3. _____ Argued that religious ideologies serve to justify the status quo and retard social change.

a. Karl Marx
b. Keith A. Roberts
c. Max Weber

Learning Objectives

After reading Chapter 17, the student should be able to:

1. define religion and list some of the elements that make up religions (p. 528).
2. be able to complete the true-false quiz on the impact of religion on education in Canada (pp. 529–30).
3. define faith, sacred, profane, and rituals and explain their role in religion (pp. 531–32).
4. list and describe the four main categories of religion (p. 532).
5. understand what Emile Durkheim considered the central feature of all religions (p. 533).
6. list and describe the three key functions of religion (pp. 533–34).

7. describe how Karl Marx viewed ideologies and explain why he considered religion to be the "opiate of the masses" (p. 534).

8. discuss Max Weber's views on religion and note how these views are similar to and different from those of Karl Marx (pp. 534–36).

9. explain how symbolic interactionists view religion as a reference and be familiar with the reasons why people convert to nontraditional religious movements (pp. 536–37).

10. explain the feminist assumption that not all people interpret religion in the same way (pp. 537–38).

11. describe the two religious issues that, according to feminists, are becoming increasingly important to women in today's society (p. 538).

12. note how postmodernists explain the co-existence of secularization in some parts of the world and increased religiosity in others (pp. 538–41).

13. define ecclesia and explain how membership occurs (p. 543).

14. list the key characteristics of churches and sects identified by Troeltsch and Weber's church–sect typology (pp. 543–44).

15. define cult and note why new religious movements develop (pp. 544–45).

16. explain why Canada is called a "monopolized mosaic" (p. 545).

17. describe major trends in Canadian religiosity (pp. 546–48).

18. note why Canadians are turning away from the church (pp. 548–50).

19. define fundamentalism and note recent trends in this area (p. 550).

20. describe major findings on the impact of religion on the attitudes and behaviour of Canadians (pp. 550–52).

Unit Mastery Quizzes

Unit Mastery – Multiple Choice

1. Religion:
   a. is a system of beliefs, symbols, and rituals based on some sacred or supernatural realm.
   b. guides human behaviour and gives meaning to life.
   c. unites believers into a community.
   d. all of the above.

2. Which of the following statements is FALSE?
   a. Few religions attempt to answer fundamental questions such as those regarding the meaning of life and how the world was created.
   b. Most religions provide comfort to persons facing emotional traumas such as illness, suffering, grief, and death.
   c. Religious beliefs are typically woven into a series of narratives, including stories about how ancestors and significant others had meaningful experiences with supernatural powers.
   d. Religion is one of the most significant social institutions in society.

3. An unquestioning belief that does not require proof of scientific evidence is known as:
    a. sacred.
    b. profane.
    c. secular.
    d. faith.

4. Sacred beliefs:
    a. have their foundation in scientific knowledge or everyday expectations.
    b. are rooted in the holy or supernatural.
    c. are the everyday, worldly aspects of life.
    d. are carefully prescribed forms of behaviour that symbolize a cherished value or belief.

5. The category of religion that contains the belief that supernatural forces affect people's lives either positively or negatively is:
    a. animism.
    b. theism.
    c. simple supernaturalism.
    d. transcendent idealism.

6. The category of religion that contains the belief in a god or gods is:
    a. animism.
    b. theism.
    c. simple supernaturalism.
    d. transcendent idealism.

7. Transcendent idealism is a _____ religion.
    a. monotheistic
    b. polytheistic
    c. nontheistic
    d. unitheistic

8. _____ typically emphasize the ways in which religious beliefs and rituals can bind people together.
    a. Functionalists
    b. Conflict theorists
    c. Symbolic interactionists
    d. Feminists

9. According to functionalists, all of the following are major functions of religion EXCEPT:
    a. providing meaning and purpose in life.
    b. promoting social cohesion and a sense of belonging.
    c. providing a reference groups from which people define themselves.
    d. providing a social control and support for the government.

10. According to Karl Marx:
    a. ideologies that are embodied in religious doctrines and political values serve to justify the status quo and retard social change.
    b. religion could be a catalyst to produce social change.
    c. the religious teachings of John Calvin were directly related to the rise of capitalism.
    d. sacred symbols and beliefs establish powerful, long-lasting motivations based on the concept of a general order of existence.

11. According to Max Weber:
    a. ideologies that are embodied in religious doctrines and political values serve to justify the status quo and retard social change.
    b. religion could be a catalyst to produce social change.
    c. religious teachings and practices help promote social cohesion.
    d. religion helps bind people together and maintain social control.

12. _____ focus their attention on a microlevel analysis that examines the meanings that people give to religion in their everyday life.
    a. Functionalists
    b. Conflict theorists
    c. Symbolic interactionists
    d. Feminists

13. According to Lofland and Stark, predisposing characteristics among religious converts include:
    a. some important tension or strain in their lives.
    b. a religious problem-solving perspective.
    c. the self-definition as religious seekers who actively sought to resolve their problems through some system of religious meaning.
    d. all of the above.

14. All of the following are situational factors that promote religious conversion according to Lofland and Stark EXCEPT:
    a. the fact that an individual had come to a turning point in his or her life at the time of encountering the Divine Precepts.
    b. affective ties with a member of the Divine Precepts.
    c. exposure to very intensive interaction with Divine Precepts members.
    d. the absence of exposure to different religious alternatives other than the Divine Precepts.

15. According to feminist perspectives:
    a. in virtually all religions, women have much less influence on the establishment of social definitions of appropriate gender roles both within the religious community and in the larger community.
    b. women's versions of particular religions probably differ remarkedly from men's versions.
    c. religious symbolism and language typically create a social definition of the roles of men and men.
    d. all of the above.

16. A religious organization that is so integrated into the dominant culture that it claims as its membership all members of a society is:
    a. the ecclesia.
    b. the church.
    c. a sect.
    d. a cult.

17. Which of the following is an issue that is becoming increasingly important to women in today's society?
    a. the absence of women in significant roles within religious institutions
    b. the gender-inclusiveness of Christianity and Judaism
    c. a and b
    d. none of the above are issues of concern in today's society

18. Canada has been described as a "monopolized mosaic" because:
    a. Protestants and Catholics have always dominated the religious population in Canada.
    b. There are equal numbers of Protestants, Catholics, and Hindus in Canada.
    c. The vast majority of Canadians are in the "other" religious category.
    d. Canadians are about equally divided among Protestant, Catholic, no religion, and other.

19. The emergence of new religious movements has been attributed to:
    a. rapid changes in social values.
    b. changes in social structure.
    c. changes in the role and character of religious institutions.
    d. all of the above.

20. Which of the following describes a major trend in religiosity in Canada?
    a. Attendance at Roman Catholic church services has increased in recent years.
    b. Attendance in mainline Protestant churches (e.g., United, Anglican) has increased in recent years.
    c. The vast majority of Canadians report a religious affiliation and affirm that they believe in God.
    d. Attendance rates have declined the most for persons aged 65 years of age and older.

Unit Mastery – True or False

1. Provincial governments in Canada do not fund separate religious schools (p. 528).

    TRUE or FALSE

2. Parents who wish to home school their children for religious reasons are free to teach the children whatever curriculum they wish (p. 530).

    TRUE or FALSE

3. The federal government has limited control over how funds are spent by school districts because most of the money comes from the provinces, thus questions of religion in the schools are decided at the provincial level (p. 530).

    TRUE or FALSE

4. Enrollment in parochial schools has decreased in Canada as interest in religion has waned (p. 530).

    TRUE or FALSE

5. In Canada, the public school system recognizes only Christian religious holidays by giving students those days off (p. 530).
TRUE or FALSE

6. The number of children from religious backgrounds other than Christian and Judaic has grown steadily in schools over the past three decades (p. 530).
TRUE or FALSE

7. Debates over textbook content focus only on elementary education because of the vulnerability of young children (p. 530).
TRUE or FALSE

8. Increasing numbers of parents are instructing their own children through home-schooling because of their concerns about what public schools are (or are not) teaching their children (p. 530).
TRUE or FALSE

9. Prayer in public schools in Canada is offered on a voluntary basis (p. 530).
TRUE or FALSE

10. Most Canadians feel that the public schools should teach children about all of the major religions in the world (p. 530).
TRUE or FALSE

Unit Mastery − Fill In the Blanks

1. People often act out their religious beliefs in the form of _____ , regularly repeated and carefully prescribed forms of behaviour that symbolize a cherished value or belief (p. 531).

2. For many people, religion serves as a _____ _____ to help them define themselves (p. 536).

3. Membership in the _____ occurs as a result of being born into a society, rather than any conscious decision on part of individual members (p. 543).

4. Midway between a church and a sect is a _____ , a large, organized religious body characterized by accommodation to society but frequently lacking the ability or intention to dominate society (p. 543).

5. According to the church− _____ typology, as members of a sect become more successful economically and socially, they tend to focus more on this world and less on the next (p. 544).

6. Until the end of the nineteenth century, Canada was a country with a religious population made up almost entirely of Protestants and _____ (p. 545).

7. In very simple preindustrial societies, religion often takes the form of simple _____ , the belief that supernatural forces affect people's lives either positively or negatively (p. 532).

8. A _____ is a religious group with practices and teaching outside the dominant cultural and religious traditions of a society (p. 544).

9. The term *religious* _____ refers to a conservative religious doctrine that opposes intellectualism and worldly accommodation in favour of restoring a traditional otherworldly focus (p. 550).

10. _____ _____ is a Christian movement that advocates freedom from political subjugation within a traditional perspective and the need for social transformation to benefit the poor and downtrodden (p. 552).

Unit Mastery – Matching Quiz

Match the concept with the appropriate theoretical perspective on religion:

1. _____ functionalist perspective
2. _____ conflict perspective
3. _____ interactionist perspective
4. _____ feminist perspective
5. _____ postmodern perspective

a. opiate of the masses
b. reference group
c. social cohesion
d. oppositional ideology
e. gender-inclusiveness

Solutions

Key Terms Quiz

Review of Key Terms – Fill In the Blanks

1. cult
2. Religion
3. Animism
4. Rituals
5. church
6. Faith
7. Nontheistic religion
8. Polytheism
9. Profane
10. Sacred
11. Monotheism
12. Simple supernaturalism
13. sect
14. Ecclesia
15. Liberation theology
16. Denomination
17. Theism

Key People Quiz

Review of Key People – Matching Quiz 1

1. D
2. B
3. A
4. C

Review of Key People – Matching Quiz 2

1. C
2. B
3. A

Unit Mastery Quizzes

Unit Mastery – Multiple Choice

1. D
2. A
3. D
4. B
5. C
6. B
7. C
8. A
9. C
10. A
11. B
12. C
13. D
14. D
15. D
16. A
17. C
18. A
19. D
20. C

Unit Mastery – True or False

1. F, Schools operated by the Catholic church are provincially funded in several provinces, and others fund a variety of private schools, including religious ones.
2. F, Every province monitors home schoolers to ensure compliance with its Education Act. However, as suggested by the Barendregts in the chapter introduction, enforcement of the law may be lax in some provinces.
3. T
4. F, In recent years, just the opposite has happened. As parents have begun feeling that their children were not receiving the type of education the parents desired for them in public schools, parochial schools have flourished.
5. T
6. T
7. F, Attempts to remove textbooks occur at all levels of schooling. Parents in many communities have tried to prevent teachers from using Harry Potter books in the classroom because they felt the books promoted witchcraft.
8. T
9. T
10. T

Unit Mastery – Fill In the Blanks

1. rituals
2. reference group
3. ecclesia
4. denomination
5. sect
6. Catholics
7. supernaturalism
8. cult
9. fundamentalism
10. Liberation theology

Unit Mastery – Matching Quiz

1. C
2. A
3. B
4. E
5. D

Health, Health Care, and Disability

Chapter Outline

I. Health and Medicine

II. Sociological Perspectives on Health and Medicine

    A. The Functionalist Perspective on Health: The Sick Role

    B. Symbolic Interactionist Theory: The Social Construction of Illness

    C. Postmodern Analysis: The Clinical Gaze

    D. Conflict Theory: Inequalities in Health and Health Care

III. Social Factors in Health: Age, Sex, and Social Class

    A. Age

    B. Sex

    C. Social Class

IV. Race, Class, and Health: Canada's Aboriginals

    A. Health Problems Among Aboriginals Peoples in Canada

    B. Aboriginal Healing Methods

V. Disability

    A. Sociological Perspectives on Disability

    B. Disability in Contemporary Society

VI. Social Development and Health: A Global Perspective

    A. Health Care in Canada

    B. Universal Health Care

    C. Health Care in the United States

VII. Approaches to Health Care

    A. The Medical Model of Illness

    B. Alternative Approaches

VIII. Health Care Issues in the Future

Chapter Summary

Health includes both the absence of disease and a positive sense of wellness. Medicine is an institutionalized system for the scientific diagnosis, treatment, and prevention of illness. Functionalist perspectives on health highlight the importance of sick roles—patterns of behaviour defined as appropriate for people who are sick—and view illness as dysfunctional for both the individual who is sick and for the larger society. In contrast, symbolic interactionists try to understand the social definition of illness and meaning of illness for the individual experiencing health problems. Foucault's postmodern perspective provides insights on medical prestige and dominance over other medical personnel and everyday people. Conflict approaches consider the political and social forces that affect health and the health care system, including the ability of all citizens to obtain health care; the impact of race, class, and gender; the relative power of doctors compared with other health workers; the dominance of the medical model of health care; and the role of profit in the health care system.

In Canada, health care is universal and is a provincial responsibility; each province has its own medical insurance plan that meets five requirements: universality, comprehensiveness, accessibility, portability, and public administration. Disability has been defined in many ways, including an inability to work, an organically based impairment, or a health condition that stigmatizes or causes discrimination. Disabilities are associated with economic hardship, inadequate government assistance programs, and negative social attitudes toward disabled persons.

As we begin the twenty-first century, AIDS is among the most significant global/human problems we face. In addition, we can expect continuance in the trend from hospital-based care to home-based care. New reproductive technologies will continue to create difficult social and ethical dilemmas for Canadians.

Key Terms

acute illness *(p. 561)*

chronic illness *(p. 562)*

disability *(p. 573)*

epidemic *(p. 571)*

health *(p. 559)*

health care *(p. 559)*

medicalization *(p. 562)*

medicine *(p. 559)*

preventive medicine *(p. 559)*

senile dementia *(p. 569)*

sick role *(p. 561)*

universal health care system *(p. 579)*

Key Terms Quiz

Review of Key Terms – Fill In the Blanks

1. _____ is the process whereby an object or a condition becomes defined by society as a physical or psychological illness.

2. _____ is the state of complete physical, mental, and social well-being.

3. _____ _____ is any activity intended to improve health.

4. _____ _____ are patterns of behaviour defined as appropriate for people who are sick.

5. _____ is an institutionalized system for the scientific diagnosis, treatment, and prevention of illness.

6. _____ _____ is medicine that emphasizes a healthy lifestyle in order to prevent poor health before it occurs.

7. _____ _____ is a term for diseases, such as Alzheimer's, that involve a progressive impairment of judgment and memory.

8. _____ _____ _____ _____ is a system in which all citizens receive medical services paid for through taxation revenues.

9. _____ _____ is a long-term or permanent condition that may or may not be fatal.

10. _____ are sudden, significant increases in the numbers of people contracting a disease.

11. _____ _____ is illness of limited duration from which the patient recovers or dies.

12. _____ is a physical or health condition that reduces a person's ability to perform tasks he or she would normally do at a given stage of life and that may result in stigmatization of or discrimination against the person.

Key People

Janice Acoose-Pelletier *(p. 572)*

Peter Conrad and Joseph Schneider *(p. 563)*

Michel Foucault *(p. 565)*

Michael Oliver *(p. 574)*

Talcott Parsons *(p. 561)*

Ingrid Waldron *(p. 569)*

Meira Weiss *(p. 575)*

Key People Quiz

Review of Key People – Matching Quiz 1

1. _____ Emphasize that many behaviours that were at one time defined as "badness" have been redefined as "sickness" or "illnesses."

2. _____ Used the term "disability oppression" to describe the barriers that exist for disabled persons in Canadian society.

3. _____ Described the problems the Western medical model has created for Aboriginal people.

4. _____ Questioned existing assumptions about medical knowledge and the power doctors have gained over other medical personnel and everyday people.

a. Janice Acoose-Pelletier
b. Peter Conrad and Joseph Schneider
c. Michel Foucault
d. Michael Oliver

Review of Key People – Matching Quiz 2

1. _____ Challenged the assumption that parents automatically bond with infants, especially those born with visible disabilities.

2. _____ Identified three factors that lead to sex differences in mortality rates.

3. _____ A functionalist who claims that all societies have a sick role in which the sick person is exempt from normal social responsibilities.

a. Talcott Parsons
b. Ingrid Waldron
c. Meira Weiss

Learning Objectives

After reading Chapter 18, the student should be able to:

1. define health, health care, medicine, and preventive medicine (p. 559).
2. list and describe the key characteristics of the sick role, as outlined by the functionalist perspective and discuss the key criticisms (pp. 559–61).
3. explain how symbolic interactionists view health as a social construction of illness (pp. 561–62).
4. define medicalization and explain what this process entails (pp. 562–64).
5. describe feminist views on the medicalization of women's lives (pp. 564–65).
6. explain what Foucault meant by the "clinical gaze" (p. 565).

7. describe how the conflict theory views inequalities in health care (pp. 565–66).

8. note the relationships between age and health and sex and health (pp. 567–69).

9. describe the relationship between social class and health (pp. 569–71).

10. note some of the reasons why Aboriginals have poorer health than non-Aboriginals (pp. 571–72).

11. explain why the Western medical model poses problems for Aboriginal healing methods (pp. 572–73).

12. understand how the term "disability" can be defined in many ways (pp. 573–76).

13. compare and contrast the sociological perspectives on disability (p. 574).

14. describe characteristics of persons most at risk for disabilities in Canada and note why disability is increasing in contemporary society (pp. 574–76).

15. note how Canada ranks globally in terms of its health care system (pp. 578–79).

16. define universal health care and describe the system in place in Canada prior to the early 1960s. (pp. 579–80).

17. list and describe key requirements for provincial health care plans (p. 581).

18. note criticisms of Canada's health care system (pp. 581–82).

19. note how health care in the United States differs from that in Canada (pp. 582–83).

20. describe the medical model of illness in Western society and describe some alternative approaches (pp. 583–85).

Unit Mastery Quizzes

Unit Mastery – Multiple Choice

1. Disability refers to:
   a. an inability to engage in gainful employment.
   b. an organically based impairment.
   c. a physical or health condition that stigmatizes or causes discrimination.
   d. all of the above are definitions of disability.

2. Any activity that is designed to improve health would be considered:
   a. medicine.
   b. health.
   c. health care.
   d. disease free.

3. Which perspective claims that the meaning that social actors give their illness will affect their own self-concept as well as relationships with others?
   a. symbolic interactionist
   b. conflict
   c. functionalist
   d. postmodern

4. The conflict approach to health care:
   a. emphasizes the meaning a person gives to his or her illness.
   b. considers the inequities that result from political and social forces.
   c. views illness as dysfunctional both for the individual who is sick and for the larger society.
   d. views the sick role as functional in helping an individual overcome illness.

5. All of the following are key characteristics of the sick role EXCEPT:
   a. The sick person is exempt from normal social responsibilities.
   b. The sick person must want to get well.
   c. The sick person should seek technically competent help and cooperate with health care practitioners.
   d. The sick person must assume responsibility for his or her condition.

6. Which of the following statements about health care in Canada is FALSE?
   a. In 1996, government funding for health care fell for the first time since the birth of medicare.
   b. For many years, the United Nations has ranked Canada one of the three best places in the world to live.
   c. Over time, Canadians are becoming increasingly satisfied with the health care system.
   d. Canadians are now experiencing longer waiting times for surgery and other medical procedures.

7. All of the following are key requirements of provincial health standards EXCEPT:
   a. All Canadians should be covered on a first-come, first-served basis.
   b. All necessary medical services should be guaranteed, without dollar limits, and should be available solely on the basis of medical need.
   c. Benefits should be transferable from province to province.
   d. Health care should be operated on a nonprofit basis by a public agency.

8. The medical model assumes that:
   a. illness is deviation from normal.
   b. illness is specific and universal.
   c. illness is caused by biological forces.
   d. all of the above.

9. The number of persons with disabilities is increasing due to:
   a. advances in medical technology that promote survival of individuals who would have formerly died from an accident or illness.
   b. increased life expectancy, which means people live long enough to experience diseases.
   c. higher survival rates of persons born with serious disabilities.
   d. all of the above.

10. _____ involves not only the absence of disease but also a positive sense of wellness.
    a. Medicine
    b. Health
    c. Health care
    d. Preventive medicine

11. Which of the following statements about HIV/AIDS is FALSE?
    a. Worldwide, most people with AIDS are gay men.
    b. HIV, the virus that transmits AIDS, is spreading rapidly among women in some nations.
    c. Nearly 50 percent of people who are HIV-positive worldwide are under the age of 25.
    d. One of the major concerns of AIDS activists is reducing the stigmatization of HIV/AIDS victims.

12. In 1989, the American Society for Plastic and Reconstructive Surgery wanted the U.S. government to loosen its restrictions on the use of breast implants based on the view that having small breasts constituted a disease. This example illustrates:
    a. demedicalization
    b. medicalization
    c. dementia
    d. portability

13. Rates of illness and death are highest among:
    a. the old.
    b. middle-aged individuals.
    c. the young.
    d. a and c.

14. The main reason behind provincial and federal governments' attempts to restructure health care is:
    a. Canada's aging society.
    b. increased infant mortality rates.
    c. funding cutbacks.
    d. health issues among Aboriginals.

15. Greater life expectancy among females can be attributed to:
    a. differences in gender roles that promote less risky behaviour in females.
    b. the fact that women are more likely to make use of the health care system.
    c. biological differences.
    d. all of the above.

16. Epidemics among Aboriginals were largely the result of:
    a. no immunity to European diseases.
    b. new patterns of trade that led to contact with more diverse groups of people.
    c. crowded reserves that lacked proper sanitation and hygiene facilities.
    d. all of the above.

17. Which of the following statements accurately describes disability in Canada?
    a. Aboriginal people have higher rates of disability than other Canadians.
    b. About 25 percent of the adult population in Canada reports having one or more physical or mental abilities.
    c. Most disabled individuals have hearing or vision impairment.
    d. Most disabled individuals of working age who receive care at home are employed.

18. Which of the following countries has the highest number of HIV-positive people?
    a. Africa
    b. Canada
    c. Asia
    d. Eastern Europe

19. Which of the following statements about universal health care is FALSE?
    a. Canadians have always had a universal health care system.
    b. In a universal health care system, medical services are paid through taxation revenues.
    c. Health care is a provincial responsibility, and each province has its own medical insurance plan.
    d. Many of the costs are controlled by doctors, who prescribe drugs, admit patients to hospitals, determine the course of treatment, and recommend follow-up visits.

20. Which of the following statements best characterizes health care in the United States?
    a. The United States has a universal health care system.
    b. The United States has a private health care system.
    c. The United States has a public health care system.
    d. The United States has a mixture of private and public health care.

Unit Mastery – True or False

1. Talcott Parsons viewed illness as dysfunctional for both the individual who is sick and for the larger society (p. 561).
   TRUE or FALSE

2. An illness that is seen primarily as infectious is perceived as dishonourable or shameful (p. 562).
   TRUE or FALSE

3. Rates of illness and death are highest among the old and the young (p. 567).
   TRUE or FALSE

4. Access to medical care improves the health of the poor (p. 570).
   TRUE or FALSE

5. Health care is a federal responsibility, and each province has the same medical insurance plan (p. 581).
   TRUE or FALSE

6. Worldwide, most people with AIDS are gay men (p. 560).
   TRUE or FALSE

7. People can get AIDS from sharing toilets, toothbrushes, eating utensils, or razors (p. 560).
   TRUE or FALSE

8. People infected with HIV may not show any physical symptoms for ten years or longer and can infect others without realizing it (p. 560).
   TRUE or FALSE

9. Infant mortality rates among Aboriginal people are nearly twice the Canadian average (p. 571).
   TRUE or FALSE

10. Under the Canadian universal system, if you are sick, you have the right to receive medical care regardless of your ability to pay (p. 580).

TRUE or FALSE

Unit Mastery – Fill In the Blanks

1. _____ refers to the process whereby an object or a condition becomes defined by society as a physical or psychological illness (p. 562).

2. Michael Oliver (1990) used the term _____ _____ to describe the barriers that exist for disabled persons in Canadian society (p. 574).

3. A _____ _____ _____ system is one in which all citizens receive medical services paid for through taxation revenues (p. 579).

4. Reasonable access to health care is referred to as _____ (p. 581).

5. A _____ approach emphasizes interdependence of body, mind, and environment (p. 584).

6. Medicine forms a vital part of the broader concept of _____ _____ , which is any activity intended to improve health (p. 558).

7. _____ _____ is a term for diseases, such as Alzheimer's, that involve a progressive impairment of judgment and memory (p. 569).

8. Sudden increases in the numbers of people contracting a disease are called _____ (p. 571).

9. A _____ may be defined as an inability to engage in gainful employment (p. 573).

10. _____ is a provincial health plan requirement that stipulates that all necessary medical services should be guaranteed (p. 581).

Unit Mastery – Matching Quiz 1

Match the description to the appropriate health care standard:

1. _____ accessibility
2. _____ portability
3. _____ universality
4. _____ public administration
5. _____ comprehensiveness

a. all Canadians should be covered
b. all necessary medical services should be guaranteed
c. reasonable access should be guaranteed
d. benefits should be transferable from province to province
e. should be operated on a nonprofit basis by a public agency

Unit Mastery − Matching Quiz 2

Match the theoretical perspective with its application to health care:

1. _____ the process of medicalization and demedicalization
2. _____ debate over the allocation of resources for research and treatment
3. _____ illness is dysfunctional both for the individual who is sick and for society
4. _____ the clinical gaze

a. postmodern perspective
b. functionalist perspective
c. conflict perspective
d. symbolic interactionist perspective

Solutions

Key Terms Quiz

Review of Key Terms – Fill In the Blanks

1. Medicalization
2. Health
3. Health care
4. Sick role
5. Medicine
6. Preventive medicine
7. Senile dementia
8. Universal health care system
9. Chronic illness
10. Epidemics
11. Acute illness
12. Disability

Key People Quiz

Review of Key People – Matching Quiz 1

1. B
2. D
3. A
4. C

Review of Key People – Matching Quiz 2

1. C
2. B
3. A

Unit Mastery Quizzes

Unit Mastery – Multiple Choice

1. D
2. C
3. A
4. B
5. D
6. C
7. A
8. D
9. D
10. B
11. A
12. B
13. D
14. A
15. D
16. D
17. A
18. A
19. A
20. D

Unit Mastery – True or False

1. T
2. T
3. T
4. T
5. F, Health care is a provincial responsibility, and each province has its own medical insurance plan.
6. F, Although AIDS has taken a devastating toll on the gay population in North America, the World Health Organization estimates that about 75 percent of the people with AIDS worldwide were infected through heterosexual intercourse.
7. F, AIDS is caused by HIV (human immunodeficiency virus), which is transmitted to men or women through unprotected sexual intercourse with an infected partner, through sharing a contaminated hypothermic needle with someone who is infected, through exposure to contaminated blood or blood products, and through the passing on the virus by an infected woman to her child during pregnancy, childbirth, or breastfeeding.
8. T
9. T
10. T

Unit Mastery – Fill In the Blanks

1. Medicalization
2. disability oppression
3. universal health care
4. accessibility
5. holistic
6. health care
7. Senile dementia
8. epidemics
9. disability
10. Comprehensiveness

Unit Mastery – Matching Quiz 1

1. C
2. E
3. A
4. D
5. B

Unit Mastery – Matching Quiz 2

1. D
2. C
3. B
4. A

Population and Urbanization

Chapter Outline

Chapter Summary

Demography is the study of the size, composition, and distribution of the population. Population growth results from fertility (births), mortality (deaths), and migration. Over two hundred years ago, Thomas Malthus warned that overpopulation would result in global poverty and starvation. According to the Marxist perspective, overpopulation occurs because of capitalist demands for a surplus of workers to suppress wages and heighten workers' productivity. Demographic transition is the process by which some societies have moved from high birth and death rates to relatively low ones as a result of technological development.

Urban sociology is the study of social relationships and political and economic structures in the city. Functionalist perspectives (ecological models) of urban growth include the concentric zone model, the sector model, and the multiple-nuclei model. According to the political economy models of conflict theorists, urban growth is influenced by capital investment decisions, power and resource inequality, class and class conflict, and government subsidy programs. Feminist theorists suggest that cities have gender regimes; women's lives are affected by both public and private patriarchy. Symbolic interactionists focus on the positive and negative aspects of peoples' experiences in the urban settings. Urbanization, suburbanization, gentrification, and the growth of edge cities have had a dramatic impact on the population. Many central cities have experienced fiscal crises that have resulted in cuts in services, lack of maintenance of the infrastructure, and a health care crisis. Postmodern societies are shaped by land developers and business owners and tend to be characterized by the private, inaccessible spaces. Rapid global population growth is inevitable and may lead to increased environmental activism.

Key Terms

central city *(p. 611)*

crude birth rate *(p. 593)*

crude death rate *(p. 594)*

demographic transition *(p. 606)*

demography *(p. 592)*

emigration *(p. 595)*

fertility *(p. 592)*

gentrification *(p. 613)*

immigration *(p. 595)*

infant mortality rate *(pp. 594 – 95)*

invasion *(p. 613)*

megalopolis *(p. 622)*

metropolis *(p. 611)*

migration *(p. 595)*

mortality *(p. 594)*

population composition *(p. 599)*

population pyramid *(p. 599)*

sex ratio *(p. 599)*

succession *(p. 613)*

urban sociology *(p. 610)*

Key Terms Quiz

Review of Key Terms – Fill In the Blanks

1. _Demography_ is the subfield of sociology that examines population size, composition, and distribution.

2. _Gentrification_ is the process by which members of the middle and upper-middle classes move into the central city area and renovate existing properties.

3. _Megalopolis_ is a continuous concentration of two or more cities and their suburbs that have grown until they form an interconnected urban area.

4. _Fertility_ is the actual level of childbearing for an individual or a population.

5. _Demographic transition_ is the process by which some societies have moved from high birth and death rates to relatively low birth and death rates as a result of technological development.

6. _Crude birth rate_ is the number of live births per 1,000 people in a population in a given year.

7. _Emigration_ is the movement of people out of a geographic area to take up residency elsewhere.

8. _Crude death rate_ is the number of deaths per 1,000 people in a population in a given year.

9. _Immigration_ is the movement of people into a geographic area to take up residency.

10. _Mortality_ is the incidence of death in a population.

11. _Infant mortality rate_ is the number of deaths of infants under one year of age per 1,000 live births in a given year.

12. _Population pyramid_ is a graphical representation of the distribution of a population by sex and age.

13. _Urban Sociology_ is a subfield of sociology that examines social relationships and political and economic structures in the city.

14. _Migration_ is the movement of people from one geographic area to another for the purpose of changing residency.

15. _Metropolis_ is one or more central cities and their surrounding suburbs that dominate the economic and cultural life of a region.

16. ___sex   ratio___ is the number of males for every hundred females in a given population.

17. ___population composition___ is the biological and social characteristics of a population.

18. ___Invasion___ is the process by which a new category of people or type of land use arrives in an area previously occupied by another group or land use.

19. ___Succession___ is the process by which a new category of people or type of land use gradually predominates an area formerly dominated by another group or activity.

20. ___Central   city___ is the densely populated centre of a metropolis.

Key People

Lynn M. Appleton *(p. 615)*

Ernest W. Burgess *(p. 612)*

Herbert Gans *(p. 616)*

Chauncey Harris and Edward Ullman *(p. 613)*

Thomas Homer-Dixon *(p. 605)*

Homer Hoyt *(p. 613)*

Thomas Robert Malthus *(p. 604)*

Karl Marx and Friedrich Engels *(p. 604)*

Robert Park *(p. 612)*

Georg Simmel *(p. 616)*

Ferdinand Tönnies *(p. 610)*

Timothy Weiskel *(p. 608)*

Elizabeth Wilson *(p. 615)*

Louis Wirth *(p. 616)*

Key People Quiz

Review of Key People – Matching Quiz 1

1. ___F___ Studied the configuration of 142 cities, and came up with a sector model that emphasizes the significance of terrain and the importance of transportation routes.

2. ___A___ Claimed that different cities have different ideas of how women and men should think, feel, and act; how access to social positions and control of resources should be managed; and how relationships between men and women should be conducted.

3. ___D___ Developed a model in which cities have numerous centres of development based on specific urban needs or activities.

4. ___C___ Claimed there are five major categories of adaptation among urban dwellers: cosmopolites, unmarried and childless couples, ethnic villagers, the deprived, and the trapped.

5. ___B___ Developed the concentric zone model to explain why some cities expand radically from a central business core.

6. ___E___ Feels that increases in population and resource consumption will lead to significant environmental changes, including climatic instability and scarcities of soil and water.

7. ___G___ Claimed that the population, if left unchecked, would exceed the available food supply.

a. Lynn M. Appleton
b. Ernest W. Burgess
c. Herbert Gans
d. Chauncey Harris and Edward Ullman
e. Thomas Homer-Dixon
f. Homer Hoyt
g. Thomas Robert Malthus

Review of Key People – Matching Quiz 2

1. __E__ Pointed out that we should not expect that developing countries will follow the same path as Western nations.

2. __B__ Claimed that economic competition produces certain regularities in land use patterns and population distributions.

3. __D__ Used the terms *Gemeinschaft* and *Gesellschaft* to characterize the degree of social integration in societies.

4. __C__ Believed that urban life is highly stimulating and shapes people's thoughts and actions.

5. __G__ Suggested that urbanization is a way of life.

6. __A__ Viewed poverty as a consequence of the exploitation of workers by the owners of the means of production.

7. __F__ Claimed that some men view the city as sexual space in which women are categorized as prostitutes, lesbians, temptresses, or virtuous women in need of protection.

a. Karl Marx and Friedrich Engels
b. Robert Park
c. Georg Simmel
d. Ferdinand Tönnies
e. Timothy Weiskel
f. Elizabeth Wilson
g. Louis Wirth

Learning Objectives

After reading Chapter 19, the student should be able to:

1. define the study of demography and be able to identify key questions of interest to demographers (p. 592).

2. define fertility and explain how biological and social factors influence the level of fertility in a society (pp. 592–94).

3. define mortality and describe the two types of mortality rates demographers most often measure (pp. 594–95).

4. define migration and identify the two forms of movement (p. 595).

5. distinguish between internal and international migration and note the major causes of migration (pp. 595–99).

6. explain how fertility, mortality, and migration affect the population composition (pp. 599–601).

7. describe the impact of the baby boom and bust on Canadian society (pp. 601–04).

8. explain the Malthusian perspective on population growth (p. 604).

9. describe the key assumptions of the Marxist perspective on population growth and compare it to the Malthusian perspective (p. 604).

10. describe the neo-Malthusian perspective on population growth and note the significance of zero population growth to this perspective (pp. 605–06).

11. discuss demographic transition theory and be able to describe the four stages of economic development (pp. 606–08).

12. note how public policy has influenced population growth in China (pp. 608–09).

13. define urban sociology and trace the historical development of cities. Be sure to identify the major characteristics of preindustrial, industrial, and postindustrial cities (pp. 610–12).

14. discuss functionalist perspectives on urbanization and outline the major ecological models of urban growth (pp. 612–13).

15. be able to define and distinguish between invasion, succession, and gentrification (p. 613).

16. note some of the key differences between Canadian and U.S. cities (pp. 613–14).

17. outline conflict perspectives on urban growth (pp. 614–15).

18. using a feminist perspective on urban studies, explain what is meant by "gender regimes" and "sexual space" (p. 615).

19. explain interactionist perspectives on urban life and note the key assumptions of the major urban theorists (pp. 616–17).

20. note how urban theorists describe postmodern cities and explain what it meant by the disappearance of public space (pp. 619–21).

Unit Mastery Quizzes

Unit Mastery – Multiple Choice

1. The movement of people from one geographic area to another for the purpose of changing residency is:
   a. migration.
   b. demographic transition.
   c. advanced industrialization.
   d. urbanization.

2. According to the Malthusian perspective, population is held in check through:
   a. mortality risks.
   b. limits to fertility.
   c. moral restraint.
   d. all of the above.

3. Which perspective re-emphasizes the dangers of overpopulation as a result of exponential growth patterns?
   a. Marxist
   b. neo-Marxist
   c. neo-Malthusian
   d. interactionist

4. Which of the following statements about demographic transition theory is TRUE?
   a. Very little population growth occurs in the advanced industrialization and urbanization stage due to low birth and death rates.
   b. Significant population growth occurs in preindustrial societies because birth rates remain very high while death rates decline.
   c. In postindustrialization, birth rates increase as the cost of raising children decreases.
   d. In the advanced industrialization and urbanization stage, children are viewed as economic assets.

5. Demographers are interested in all of the following questions EXCEPT:
   a. Why does the population grow rapidly in some nations?
   b. What are the consequences of low birth rate in industrialized countries?
   c. What effect might a widespread AIDS crisis have on world population?
   d. all of the above are questions of interest to demographers.

6. Which perspective views poverty and overpopulation as a consequence of the exploitation of workers by the owners of the means of production?
   a. Mathusian
   b. Marxist
   c. neo-Marxist
   d. interactionist

7. All of the following factors affect fertility EXCEPT:
   a. the general health and level of nutrition of women of childbearing age.
   b. prevalent viewpoints regarding what constitutes the "ideal" family size.
   c. substantial increases in life expectancy.
   d. roles available to women in a society.

8. The primary cause of world population growth is:
   a. an increase in fertility.
   b. a decline in mortality.
   c. constant international migration.
   d. a diverse population composition.

9. China has:
   a. dramatically increased its rate of population growth due to changes in the economy.
   b. dramatically increased its rate of population growth due to child incentive policies.
   c. dramatically decreased its rate of population due to low family incomes.
   d. dramatically decreased its rate of population due to a one-child-per-family policy.

10. What proportion of Canadian society is considered urban?
    a. 50 percent
    b. 60 percent
    c. 70 percent
    d. 80 percent

11. Gentrification is the process by which:
    a. members of the upper and middle classes move into the central city and renovate existing properties.
    b. a new category of people or type of land use arrives in an area previously occupied by another group or land use.
    c. a new category of people or type of land use gradually predominates in an area formerly dominated by another group or activity.
    d. some societies have moved from high birth rates and death rates to relatively low birth and death rates as a result of technological development.

12. In which ecological model does invasion and succession processes play an important role?
    a. concentric zone
    b. multiple nuclei
    c. gender regimes
    d. sector

13. According to _____ perspectives, cities offer a paradox for women: on one hand, they offer more freedom than is found in comparatively isolated rural, suburban, and domestic settings; on the other, women many be in greater physical danger in the city.
    a. conflict
    b. functionalist
    c. feminist
    d. postmodernist

14. For decades, people from the Atlantic provinces moved to Ontario in search of work. This illustrates:
    a. internal migration.
    b. international migration.
    c. demographic transition.
    d. urbanization.

15. The age and sex composition of the population affects:
    a. fertility.
    b. mortality.
    c. migration.
    d. all of the above.

16. The view that not everyone experiences life the same way and that personal characteristics can affect lifestyle choices is central to which perspective?
    a. conflict
    b. Malthusian
    c. symbolic interactionist
    d. structural functionalist

17. Functionalist (economic) models include all of the following EXCEPT:
    a. concentric zone.
    b. multiple nuclei.
    c. gender regimes.
    d. sector.

18. Which of the following statements about the baby boom and bust is FALSE?
    a. The baby boom was caused by young couples who married and began having children in the years immediately following World War II.
    b. Canadian families need to have fewer children in order to compensate for trends created by baby boomers.
    c. University enrollments and crime rates had begun to decline by the 1990s.
    d. The baby boomers have always constituted the largest age group in Canadian society.

19. _____ perspectives point out that urban patterns result from basic economic processes such as capital accumulation.
    a. Conflict
    b. Functionalist
    c. Symbolic interactionist
    d. Malthusian

20. Which of the following statements concerning population trends is FALSE?
    a. Mass urbanization in North America has created a territorial division of interests between cities and suburban areas.
    b. Starvation will be less and less of a problem in developing nations due to the economic aid of North America.
    c. Although death rates have declined in many developing nations, birth rates have not correspondingly decreased.
    d. HIV/AIDS may reach epidemic proportions.

Unit Mastery − True or False

1. The presence of others from one's former home plays little or no role in determining where new immigrants settle in Canada (p. 591).

   TRUE or FALSE

2. The level of fertility in a society is based on biological and social factors (p. 592).

   TRUE or FALSE

3. Countries with high birth rates also have high infant mortality rates (p. 595).

   TRUE or FALSE

4. Migration affects the size and distribution of a population in a given area (p. 595).

   TRUE or FALSE

5. Immigration is the movement of people out of a geographic area to take up residence elsewhere (p. 595).

   TRUE or FALSE

6. The baby boom and bust has had very little impact on the age structure of Canadian society (p. 601).
    TRUE or FALSE

7. Canada's fertility is now 2.1 children per woman, which will provide replacement of our population (p. 604).
    TRUE or FALSE

8. According to the Marxist perspective, it is possible to produce the food and other goods needed to meet the demands of a growing population (p. 604).
    TRUE or FALSE

9. Invasion is the process by which a new category of people gradually predominates in an area formerly dominated by another group (p. 613).
    TRUE or FALSE

10. Compared to cities in the United States, Canadian cities are higher in density, meaning they have less urban sprawl (pp. 613–14).
    TRUE or FALSE

Unit Mastery – Fill In the Blanks

1. Demographers define **population** as a group of people who live in a specified geographical area (p. 592).

2. **Migration** refers to movement from one place to another (p. 592).

3. The most basic measure of fertility is the **Crude birth rate**, the number of live births per 1,000 people in a population in a given year (p. 593).

4. Our declining mortality rates have led to substantial increases in **life expectancy** which is an estimate of the average lifetime in years of people born in a specific year (p. 595).

5. A **metropolis** is one or more central cities and their surrounding suburbs that dominate the economic and cultural life of a region (p. 611).

6. According to the **multiple nuclei model** developed by urban ecologists Harris and Ullman (1945), cities do not have one centre from which all growth radiates, but rather they have numerous centres of development (p. 613).

7. Hoyt's **sector** model emphasizes the significance of terrain and the importance of transportation routes in the layout of cities (p. 613).

8. **Urbanism** refers to the distinctive social and psychological patterns of life typically found in the city (p. 616).

9. According to Herbert Gans, Cosmopolites are students, artists, writers, musicians, entertainers, and professionals who live in the city because they want to be close to its cultural facilities (p. 616).

10. By 2010, Rio de Janeiro and Sao Paulo are expected to have a combined population of about 40 million people living in a 500-kilometre-long megalopolis (pp. 621–22).

Unit Mastery – Matching Quiz 1

Match the central feature to its corresponding ecological model:

1. _____ concentric zone model
2. _____ sector model
3. _____ multiple nuclei model

a. invasion and succession
b. terrain and transportation
c. many centres of development

Unit Mastery – Matching Quiz 2

Match the central feature to its corresponding concentric zone:

1. _____ Zone 1
2. _____ Zone 2
3. _____ Zone 3
4. _____ Zone 4
5. _____ Zone 5

a. central business district
b. working-class residences
c. populated by commuters
d. affluent families
e. transition

Unit Mastery – Matching Quiz 3

Match the characteristic with the appropriate theoretical perspective:

1. _____ postmodern perspective
2. _____ feminist perspective
3. _____ symbolic interactionist perspective
4. _____ conflict perspective
5. _____ functionalist perspective

a. disappearance of public space
b. gender regimes in cities
c. urbanism as a way of life
d. capitalism and urban growth
e. concentric zone model

Solutions

Key Terms Quiz

Review of Key Terms – Fill In the Blanks

1. Demography
2. Gentrification
3. Megalopolis
4. Fertility
5. Demographic transition
6. Crude birth rate
7. Emigration
8. Crude death rate
9. Immigration
10. Mortality
11. Infant mortality rate
12. Population pyramid
13. Urban sociology
14. Migration
15. Metropolis
16. Sex ratio
17. Population composition
18. Invasion
19. Succession
20. Central city

Key People Quiz

Review of Key People – Matching Quiz 1

1. F
2. A
3. D
4. C
5. B
6. E
7. G

Review of Key People – Matching Quiz 2

1. E

2. B
3. D
4. C
5. G
6. A
7. F

Unit Mastery Quizzes

Unit Mastery – Multiple Choice

1. A
2. D
3. C
4. A
5. D
6. B
7. C
8. B
9. D
10. D
11. A
12. A
13. C
14. A
15. D
16. C
17. C
18. B
19. A
20. B

Unit Mastery – True or False

1. F, The presence of others from one's former home play a large role in determining where new immigrants settle in Canada. Toronto and Vancouver have very high proportions of recent immigrants.
2. T

3. T
4. T
5. F, Emigration is the movement of people out of an area while immigration is the movement of people into an area.
6. F, The baby boom and bust has had a dramatic impact on the age structure, which can be seen in the population pyramid for Canada.
7. F, Canada's fertility is near it's all time low of 1.5 children per woman, which will not provide replacement of our population.
8. T
9. F, Succession is the process whereby a new category of people gradually predominates while invasion is a process by which a new category of people arrives in an area previously occupied by another group.
10. T

Unit Mastery – Fill In the Blanks

1. population
2. Migration
3. crude birth rate
4. life expectancy
5. metropolis
6. multiple nuclei model
7. sector
8. Urbanism
9. cosmopolites
10. megalopolis

Unit Mastery – Matching Quiz 1

1. A
2. B
3. C

Unit Mastery − Matching Quiz 2

1. A
2. E
3. B
4. D
5. C

Unit Mastery − Matching Quiz 3

1. A
2. B
3. C
4. D
5. E

Collective Behaviour, Social Movements, and Social Change

Chapter Outline

I. Collective Behaviour
   A. Conditions for Collective Behaviour
   B. Dynamics of Collective Behaviour
   C. Distinctions Regarding Collective Behaviour
   D. Types of Crowd Behaviour
   E. Explanations of Crowd Behaviour
   F. Mass Behaviour

II. Social Movements
   A. Types of Social Movements
   B. Stages in Social Movements

III. Social Movement Theories
   A. Relative Deprivation Theory
   B. Value-Added Theory
   C. Resource Mobilization Theory
   D. Social Constructionist Theory: Frame Analysis
   E. New Social Movement Theory

IV. Social Change in the Future
   A. The Physical Environment and Change
   B. Population and Change
   C. Technology and Change
   D. Social Institutions and Change

V. A Few Final Thoughts

Chapter Summary

Social change is the alteration, modification, or transformation of public policy, culture, or social institutions over time. Such change usually is brought about by collective behaviour (voluntary, often spontaneous activity that is engaged in by a large number of people and typically violates dominant group norms and values).

A crowd is a relatively large number of people who are in one another's immediate vicinity. Five categories of crowds have been identified: (1) casual crowds are relatively large gatherings of people who happen to be in the same place at the same time; (2) conventional crowds comprise people who come together specifically for a scheduled event and thus share a common focus; (3) expressive crowds provide opportunities for the expression of some strong emotion; (4) acting crowds are collectivities so intensely focused on a specific purpose or object that they may erupt into violent or destructive behaviour; and (5) protest crowds are gatherings of people who engage in activities intended to achieve specific political goals. Protest crowds sometimes participate in civil disobedience (nonviolent action that seeks to change a policy or law by refusing to comply with it). Explanations of crowd behaviour include contagion theory, social unrest and circular reaction, convergence theory, and emergent norm theory.

Examples of mass behaviour include rumours, gossip, mass hysteria, fads, fashions, and public opinion. The major types of social movements are reform movements, revolutionary movements, religious movements, alternative movements, and resistance movements. Sociological theories explaining social movements include relative deprivation theory, value-added theory, resource mobilization theory, social constructionist theory, and new social movement theory.

Social change produces many challenges that need to be resolved: environmental problems, changes in the demographics of the population, and new technology that benefits some but not all people. As we continue into the twenty-first century, we must use our sociological imaginations to help resolve these problems.

Key Terms

civil disobedience *(p. 633)*

collective behaviour *(p. 629)*

crowd *(p. 631)*

environmental racism *(p. 646)*

fad *(p. 639)*

fashion *(p. 639)*

gossip *(p. 637)*

mass *(p. 631)*

mass behaviour *(p. 637)*

mass hysteria *(p. 637)*

mob *(p. 632)*

panic *(p. 632)*

propaganda *(p. 640)*

public opinion *(p. 640)*

riot *(p. 632)*

rumours *(p. 637)*

social change *(p. 628)*

social movement *(p. 641)*

terrorism *(p. 642)*

Key Terms Quiz

Review of Key Terms — Fill In the Blanks

1. A __riot__ is violent crowd behaviour that is fueled by deep-seated emotions but not directed at one specific target.

2. __Collective behaviour__ is voluntary, often spontaneous activity that is engaged in by a large number of people and typically violates dominant group norms and values.

3. A __mass__ is a number of people who share an interest in a specific idea or issue but who are not in one another's immediate vicinity.

4. A __mob__ is a highly emotional crowd whose members engage in, or are ready to engage in, violence against a specific target, a person, a category of people, or physical property.

5. __Fashion__ is currently valued style of behaviour, thinking, or appearance.

6. __Terrorism__ is the calculated unlawful use of physical force or threats of violence against persons or property in order to intimidate or coerce a government, organization, or individual for the purpose of gaining some political, religious, economic, or social objective.

7. A __crowd__ is a relatively large number of people who are in one another's immediate vicinity.

8. __Civil disobedience__ is nonviolent action that seeks to change a policy or law by refusing to comply with it.

9. __Rumours__ are unsubstantiated reports on an issue or subject.

10. A __fad__ is a temporary but widely copied activity enthusiastically followed by large numbers of people.

11. __Mass behaviour__ is collective behaviour that takes place when people (who are often geographically separated from one another) respond to the same event in much the same way.

12. __Public opinion__ consists of the political attitudes and beliefs communicated by ordinary citizens to decision makers.

13. __Panic__ is a form of crowd behaviour that occurs when a large number of people react to a real or perceived threat with strong emotions and self-destructive behaviour.

14. __Gossip__ is rumours about the personal lives of individuals.

15. Propoganda is information provided by individuals or groups that have a vested interest in furthering their own cause or damaging an opposing one.

16. mass hysteria is a form of dispersed collective behaviour that occurs when a large number of people react with strong emotions and self-destructive behaviour to a real or perceived threat.

17. Social change is the alteration, modification, or transformation of public policy, culture, or social institutions over time.

18. A social movement is an organized group that acts consciously to promote or resist change through collective action.

19. Environmental racism is the belief that a disproportionate number of hazardous facilities (including industries such as waste disposal/treatment of chemical plants) are placed in low-income areas populated primarily by people of colour.

Key People

Herbert Blumer *(p. 640)*

Lory Britt *(p. 642)*

Steven M. Buechler *(p. 647)*

Stella M. Capek *(p. 646)*

Kai Erikson *(p. 641)*

William Gamson *(p. 646)*

Gustave Le Bon *(p. 633)*

Clark McPhail and Ronald T. Wohlstein *(p. 632)*

William Ogburn *(p. 649)*

Georg Simmel *(p. 640)*

Neal Smelser *(p. 644)*

Ralph Turner and Lewis Killian *(p. 636)*

Thorstein Veblen *(p. 640)*

Key People Quiz

Review of Key People − Matching Quiz 1

1. __A___ Suggested that people in the middle and lower classes follow fashion because it is fashion, not because they desire to emulate the elite class.

2. __B___ Suggested that some movements arise specifically to alter social responses to and definitions of stigmatized attributes.

3. __E___ Describes disasters caused by technology a "new species of trouble."

4. __D___ Investigated a contaminated landfill claim and found that residents were able to mobilize for change and win a federal buyout and relocation.

5. __C___ Argued that theories pertaining to twenty-first century social movements should be oriented toward the structural, macrolevel contexts in which movements arise.

a. Herbert Blumer
b. Lory Britt
c. Steven M. Buechler
d. Stella M. Capek
e. Kai Erikson

Review of Key People – Matching Quiz 2

1. __G__ Developed the emergent norm theory.
2. __E__ Suggested a "trickle-down" theory of fashion.
3. __A__ Believed that social movements borrow, modify, or create frames as they seek to advance their goals.
4. __H__ Asserted that fashion served mainly to institutionalize conspicuous consumption among the wealthy.
5. __B__ Argued that people are more likely to engage in antisocial behaviour in a crowd because they are anonymous and feel invulnerable.
6. __C__ Added protest crowds to the four types of crowds identified by Blumer.
7. __D__ Claimed that when a change in the material culture occurs in society, a period of cultural lag follows in which the nonmaterial culture has not caught up with material development.
8. __F__ Developed the value-added theory.

a. William Gamson
b. Gustave Le Bon
c. Clark McPhail and Ronald T. Wohlstein
d. William Ogburn
e. Georg Simmel
f. Neal Smelser
g. Ralph Turner and Lewis Killian
h. Thorstein Veblen

Learning Objectives

After reading Chapter 20, the student should be able to:

1. define collective behaviour and describe the conditions necessary for such behaviour to occur (pp. 629–30).
2. list and describe the three questions that help us understand the dynamics of collective behaviour (pp. 630–31).
3. distinguish between crowds and masses (p. 631).
4. define and distinguish between casual, conventional, expressive, acting, and protest crowds (pp. 631–33).
5. discuss the key assumptions of contagion theory (p. 633).
6. explain how social unrest and circular reaction further our understanding of collective behaviour (p. 633).
7. discuss the key assumptions of convergence theory (p. 636).
8. discuss the key assumptions of emergent norm theory (pp. 636–37).

9. compare and contrast the key components of contagion, circular reaction, convergence, and emergent norm theories (pp. 633–37).

10. define mass behaviour and distinguish between the most frequent types of mass behaviour (pp. 637–41).

11. describe social movements and note when and where they are most likely to develop (pp. 641–42).

12. differentiate among the five major types of social movements based on their goals and the amount of change they seek to produce (pp. 642–43).

13. describe the stages of development in the formation of social movements (p. 643).

14. discuss the key assumptions of relative deprivation theory (p. 644).

15. discuss the six conditions of value-added theory that are used as an explanation of why people join social movements (p. 644).

16. state the key assumptions of resource mobilization theory (p. 645).

17. state the key assumptions of social constructionist theory (pp. 645–46).

18. describe new social movement theory (pp. 646–47).

19. be able to differentiate between relative deprivation theory, value-added theory, resource mobilization theory, social constructionist theory, and new social movement theory (p. 647).

20. describe the effects of physical environment, population trends, technological development, and social institutions on social change (pp. 648–51).

[handwritten note in left margin: Get Class to Do]

Unit Mastery Quizzes

Unit Mastery – Multiple Choice

1. All of the following are major contributors to collective behaviour EXCEPT:
   a. structural factors including larger causes.
   b. timing.
   c. clearly established norms.
   d. a breakdown in social control.

2. Recent social movement theories based on a symbolic interactionist perspective focus on:
   a. how social movements arise as a response to people's perceptions that they have been deprived of their fair share.
   b. the importance of the symbolic presentation of a problem to both participants and the general public.
   c. structural conduciveness and structural strain.
   d. the variety of resources that must be mobilized as well as the linkages of social movements to other groups.

3. Which of the following statements is FALSE according to value-added theory?
   a. When a society is unable to meet people's expectations that something should be done about the problem, strain occurs in the system.
   b. For a movement to develop, there must be a clear statement of the problem.
   c. To reinforce the existing generalized belief, a dramatic event must occur.
   d. A movement is most likely if there is a high level of social control on the part of law enforcement officials or political leaders.

4. Which of the following is a key question that helps us understand collective behaviour?
   a. How do people come to transcend or bypass established institutional patterns and structures?
   b. How do people's actions compare with their attitudes?
   c. Why do people act collectively rather than alone?
   d. All of the above questions help us understand collective behaviour.

5. Which theory claims that social movements are most likely to occur when an upswing in the standard of living is followed by a period of decline, such that people have unfulfilled rising expectations?
   a. relative deprivation theory
   b. value-added theory
   c. resource mobilization theory
   d. environmental justice theory

6. Which theory is based on the belief that participants in social movements are rational people who gather, use, and trade goods in order to advance their cause?
   a. relative deprivation theory
   b. value-added theory
   c. resource mobilization theory
   d. environmental justice theory

7. Religious services, graduation ceremonies, concerts, and college classes are examples of:
   a. casual crowds.
   b. conventional crowds.
   c. expressive crowds.
   d. active crowds.

8. A number of people who share an interest in a specific issue but are not in one another's immediate vicinity make up a:
   a. crowd.
   b. mass.
   c. aggregate.
   d. none of the above.

9. Fire bombings and hate crimes that are directed against a specific target by a highly emotional crowd are examples of:
   a. mob behaviour.
   b. riots.
   c. panic.
   d. civil disobedience.

10. This theory focuses on the social-psychological aspects of collective behaviour and attempts to explain how moods, attitudes, and behaviour are rapidly communicated.
    a. contagion
    b. convergence
    c. panic
    d. civil disobedience

11. In addition to collective behaviour and social movements, this chapter discusses _____ as a major contributor to social change.
    a. the physical environment
    b. changes in population size, distribution, and composition
    c. technology
    d. all of the above are discussed as sources of social change

12. Which of the following statements concerning stages in social movements is TRUE?
    a. In the preliminary stage, people begin to organize and publicize the problem.
    b. In the institutionalization stage, people begin to become aware of a problem.
    c. In the preliminary stage, widespread unrest is present.
    d. In the institutionalization stage, leaders emerge to agitate others.

13. Which theory assumes that some people have a predisposition to participate in collectivities with like-minded persons with whom they can express themselves?
    a. contagion
    b. convergence
    c. emergent norm
    d. social constructionist

14. Turner and Killian's emergent norm theory is used to explain:
    a. the shared emotions, goals, and beliefs many people bring to crowd behaviour.
    b. how a crowd takes on a life of its own as a result of anonymity.
    c. how moods, attitudes, and behaviour are communicated rapidly and why they are accepted by others.
    d. how individuals in a given collectivity develop an understanding of what is going on.

15. Which theory highlights the importance of anonymity and deindividuation in the development of a collective mind?
    a. contagion
    b. social unrest
    c. convergence
    d. emergent norm

16. An organized group that acts consciously to promote or resist change through collective action is:
    a. a social order.
    b. a social movement.
    c. a mob.
    d. a riot.

17. A movement that seeks to remake the entire system by replacing existing institutions with new ones is a(n):
    a. reform movement.
    b. revolutionary movement.
    c. religious movement.
    d. alternative movement.

18. Which theory claims that social movements result from the discontent that people feel when they compare their achievements with those of similarly situated persons and find that they have less than they think they deserve?
    a. relative deprivation theory
    b. value-added theory
    c. resource mobilization theory
    d. new social movement theory

19. All of the following are examples of mass behaviour EXCEPT:
    a. public opinion.
    b. rumours and gossip.
    c. mass hysteria and panic.
    d. protest crowds.

20. Stories that concern the personal lives of individuals that are often reported in tabloids such as the *National Enquirer* or *People* magazine represent:
    a. rumours.
    b. gossip.
    c. public opinion.
    d. urban legends.

Unit Mastery − True or False

1. A riot is a form of crowd behaviour that occurs when a large number of people react to a real or perceived threat with strong emotions and self-destructive behaviour (p. 632).
   TRUE or FALSE

2. Riots are often triggered by fear, anger, and hostility (p. 632).
   TRUE or FALSE

3. Protest crowds engage in activities intended to achieve specific political goals (pp. 632–33).
   TRUE or FALSE

4. Gustave Le Bon argued that people are more likely to engage in antisocial behaviour in a crowd because they are anonymous and feel invulnerable (p. 633).
   TRUE or FALSE

5. Research based on the social constructionist perspective often investigates how problems are framed and what names they are given (p. 645).
   TRUE or FALSE

244

6. Emergent norms occur when people define a new situation as highly unusual or see a long-standing situation in a new light (p. 636).
   (TRUE) or FALSE

7. Collective behaviour is longer lasting and more organized than social movements (p. 641).
   TRUE or (FALSE)

8. Social movements are more likely to develop in industrialized societies than in preindustrial societies (p. 641).
   (TRUE) or FALSE

9. Members of reform movements usually work within the existing system to attempt to change existing public policy so that it more adequately reflects their own value systems (p. 642).
   (TRUE) or FALSE

10. Smelser's value-added theory tends to underemphasize the importance of resources in social movements (p. 645).
    (TRUE) or FALSE

Unit Mastery − Fill In the Blanks

1. _Convergence_ theory focuses on the shared emotions, goals, and beliefs many people bring to crowd behaviour (p. 636).

2. _Conventional crowds_ are made up of people who specifically come together for a scheduled event and thus share a common focus (p. 632).

3. _Expressive Crowds_ are collectivities that provide opportunities for the expression of some strong emotion (such as joy, excitement, or grief) (p. 632).

4. Mobs, riots, and panics are examples of _acting_ crowds, collectivities so intensely focused on a specific purpose or object that they may erupt into violent or destructive behaviour (p. 632).

5. Protest crowds sometimes take the form of _civil disobidence_ in which nonviolent action is taken in an attempt to change a policy or law by refusing to comply with it (p. 633).

6. According to Robert E. Park, social unrest is transmitted through a process of _circular reaction_, the interactive communication between persons such that the discontent of one person is communicated to another, who, in turn, reflects the discontent back to the first person (p. 633).

7. Unlike contagion and convergence theories _emergent norm theory_ emphasizes the importance of social norms in shaping crowd behaviour (p. 636).

8. Whereas rumours deal with an issue or a subject, _gossip_ refers to rumours about the personal lives of individuals (p. 637).

9. Movements seeking to bring about a total change in society are referred to as <u>revolutionary movements</u> (p. 642).

10. Movements that seek limited change in some aspect of people's behaviour such as abstinence from drinking alcohol are referred to as <u>alternative movements</u> (p. 643).

Unit Mastery – Matching Quiz 1

Match the example with the appropriate type of crowd:

1. <u>B</u> casual
2. <u>A</u> conventional
3. <u>C</u> expressive
4. <u>D</u> acting
5. <u>E</u> protest

a. scheduled events
b. shoppers in a mall
c. worshippers or mourners
d. mobs and riots
e. civil disobedience

Unit Mastery – Matching Quiz 2

Match the concept with the appropriate theory of collective behaviour:

1. <u>B</u> contagion theory
2. <u>A</u> convergence theory
3. <u>C</u> emergent norm theory

a. common attributes
b. deindividuation
c. definition of the situation

Unit Mastery – Matching Quiz 3

Match the concept with the corresponding theory about social movement:

1. <u>A</u> relative deprivation theory
2. <u>C</u> value-added theory
3. <u>B</u> resource mobilization theory
4. <u>E</u> social constructionist theory
5. <u>D</u> new social movement theory

a. unfulfilled rising expectations
b. rational decision making
c. structural conduciveness
d. environmental racism
e. prognostic framing

Solutions

Key Terms Quiz

Review of Key Terms – Fill In the Blanks

1. riot
2. Collective behaviour
3. mass
4. mob
5. Fashion
6. Terrorism
7. crowd
8. Civil disobedience
9. Rumours
10. fad
11. Mass behaviour
12. Public opinion
13. Panic
14. Gossip
15. Propaganda
16. Mass hysteria
17. Social change
18. social movement
19. Environmental racism

Key People Quiz

Review of Key People – Matching Quiz 1

1. A
2. B
3. E
4. D
5. C

Review of Key People – Matching Quiz 2

1. G
2. E
3. A
4. H
5. B

6. C
7. D
8. F

Unit Mastery Quizzes

Unit Mastery – Multiple Choice

1. C
2. B
3. D
4. D
5. A
6. C
7. B
8. B
9. A
10. A
11. D
12. C
13. B
14. D
15. A
16. B
17. B
18. A
19. D
20. B

Unit Mastery – True or False

1. F, A panic occurs when people react to a threat with strong emotions. A riot refers to violent crowd behaviour fuelled by deep-seated emotions but not directed at one specific target.
2. T
3. T
4. T
5. T
6. T

7. F, Collective behaviour is short-lived and relatively unorganized.
8. T
9. T
10. T

Unit Mastery – Fill In the Blanks

1. Convergence
2. Conventional crowds
3. Expressive crowds
4. acting
5. civil disobedience
6. circular reaction
7. emergent norm theory
8. gossip
9. revolutionary movements
10. alternative movements

Unit Mastery – Matching Quiz 1

1. B
2. A
3. C
4. D
5. E

Unit Mastery – Matching Quiz 2

1. B
2. A
3. C

Unit Mastery – Matching Quiz 3

1. A
2. C
3. B
4. E
5. D